D0344308

The Tremendous World I Have Inside My Head

Atlas & Co.
New York

The Tremendous World I Have Inside My Head

*Franz Kafka:
A Biographical Essay*

Louis Begley

for Anka

Atlas & Co. *Publishers*
15 West 26th Street, 2nd floor
New York, NY 10010
www.atlasandco.com

Distributed to the trade by W. W. Norton & Company

Printed in the United States

For credit information, please see page 223

Atlas & Company books may be purchased for educational,
business, or sales promotional use. For information, please
write to info@atlasandco.com.

Library of Congress Cataloging-in-Publication Data
is available upon request

ISBN-13: 978-1-934633-06-9

13   12   11   10   09   08   1   2   3   4   5   6

Introduction

Millions have read the novels and short stories of Franz Kafka—his works have been translated into all languages with a written literature—and many more millions who have never read a line of Kafka know his name as well and find it natural to refer to their bewildering or frustrating experiences with the complexities of modern life as "Kafkaesque." Kafka himself allowed only a few of his works to be published during his lifetime. They included two novellas, *The Metamorphosis* and *In the Penal Colony*, each of which standing alone would have entitled him to an estimable rank in the literary pantheon, and a handful of short stories of equally high quality, among them "The Judgment," "A Country Doctor," "A Report to the Academy," "A Hunger Artist," and "Josephine the Singer, or the Mouse Folk," the last text he was to write. These works secured for him the admiration of an audience of writers and critics in Prague, Berlin, and Vienna, who recognized him as one of the masters of modern German prose; his work was anthologized while he was still alive, and it appeared in Czech, Hungarian, and Swedish translations. However, it is safe to say that Kafka would not have attained his towering renown without the tireless efforts of his closest friend and first biographer, Max Brod, who brought about the posthumous publication of his novels and other fiction.

Kafka left no will. But directly after Kafka's death, Brod found in his desk at his parents' apartment a letter in which Kafka enjoined him, as his last request, to burn all his writings without reading them—diaries, manuscripts, letters (those he had written and those he had received), as well as sketches—Kafka drew very well—and also all such writings of his as others might possess. With respect to papers in the hands of others, Brod was instructed to "ask for them in my name. Letters which they do not want to hand over to you, they should at least promise faithfully to burn themselves." An earlier letter to Brod, also found in Kafka's desk, went further:

> Of all my writings the only books that can stand are these: "The Judgment," "Metamorphosis," "Penal Colony," "A Country Doctor" and the short story "Hunger Artist." (The few copies of *Meditation* can remain. I do not want to give anyone the trouble of pulping them; but nothing in that volume must be printed again.) (*T*, 266)[1]

Brod chose not to follow Kafka's instructions. He based his decision partly on a 1921 conversation, in the course of which he had told Kafka that it was not his intention to destroy the papers. Brod argued that Kafka's failure after that warning to select as executor someone else who would have agreed to act in accordance with his wishes could be taken to signify that his friend was not "absolutely and finally determined that his instructions should stand." The weightier and more compelling reason was Brod's conviction that "Kafka's unpublished work contains the most wonderful treasures, and measured against his own work, the best things he has written." (*T*, 269)

---

[1] The Key to References appears at the end of this text.

However much one believes that it is the writer's absolute prerogative to decide which of his works are to be published, and which are never to see the light of day, one must be grateful that the novels and the late short stories have survived.

The clause in Kafka's second letter, authorizing Brod to recover papers from others, turned out to be of vital importance. Since 1920 Brod had in his possession the manuscript of *The Trial* and since 1923 that of *The Castle*. However, he used the second letter as a lever to obtain from Kafka's parents personal papers that were still in his room, including the inordinately long (approximately one hundred handwritten pages) *Letter to His Father*, written in 1919. From Dora Diamant (1898–1952), a young Polish-Jewish woman with whom Kafka lived in Berlin during the last months of his life, Brod obtained a sketchbook, the manuscript of the short story "The Burrow," and the last notebook of Kafka's diaries. From Milena Jesenská (1896–1944), Kafka's great love, Brod received the manuscript of *Amerika* and fifteen notebooks containing diaries from their beginning through January 6, 1921, which Kafka had given her in October 1921. Letters and more sketches, as well as the manuscript of "Josephine, the Singer," came from Robert Klopstock (1899–1972), a medical student who had contracted tuberculosis during his military service. Kafka befriended Klopstock while they were both staying at a sanatorium in Matliary, in the high Tatras (the mountain range that is the natural border between Slovakia and Poland). Klopstock had helped Dora nurse Kafka through his last illness.

Having assembled the manuscripts, Brod overcame very difficult editorial problems posed by their disorganized condition as well as Kafka's methods of composition, and fought relentlessly for the publication of the entire oeuvre. The succès d'estime Kafka's writings had enjoyed was not sufficient encouragement for German publishers to take large commercial risks—especially in view of the terrible economic conditions in Germany—on an author who hadn't sold well and whose appeal to the general public seemed limited. Nonetheless, the three novels were published in Germany: *The Trial* in 1925 (by the avant-garde Verlag Die Schmiede), *The Castle* in 1926, and *Amerika* in 1927 (both by Kurt Wolff Verlag). The prospects for Jewish writers worsened radically when Hitler came to power on January 30, 1933. Kafka's books were publicly burned. In October 1935, they were placed on the infamous "List of Harmful and Undesirable Literature." Thereafter, Brod resorted to a variety of stratagems, including an assignment of German rights to Kafka's works to Mercy Verlag in Prague. Mercy Verlag was nominally Czech although connected with the Schocken publishing firm. In 1937, the complete works were published by Mercy in the original German. The new edition included fiction that had previously existed only in manuscripts; the diaries; and some letters to friends (principally Brod) and others, but none of the letters to Felice Bauer (1887–1960), his first fiancée, or Milena Jesenská. Also in 1937, the same publishing house brought out in German Brod's biography of Kafka. (It is a shocking example of the deadening impact of the long Communist rule on Czech culture that the complete works of Kafka in Czech translation became available only in the fall of 2007.)

Kafka's diaries presented a special challenge, since he regularly wrote successive versions of his short fiction in some of the same notebooks that he used for his diary. Brod excerpted the most advanced drafts for publication. That left open the question of the appropriate treatment of the balance of the diaries. Brod's decision to publish them, and to publish as well most of Kafka's letters that had come into his possession, is far more difficult to justify than his decision to publish the unfinished fiction. There is much dazzling writing in the diaries and the letters, and without doubt they reveal much of the tormented inner life of this intensely private genius. The nature of those revelations, however, added to Kafka's request they be burned unread, should have been conclusive reason for honoring Kafka's wishes. The argument that Brod put forward to justify preserving and publishing the unfinished work—that, measured against his published work, it contained some of the best things Kafka had written—could not have been asserted by him in the case of the personal papers. In reality, the diaries are a skimpy record of Kafka's life and say relatively little of significance about most important events or the ethical, literary, or political issues of the day. As for the correspondence, Kafka's characterization (in a moment of despondency) of the letters that he and Milena exchanged is not far off the mark for many of them, and applies with even greater force to many of the letters to Felice:

> It turns out we really do keep writing the same thing. Sometimes I ask whether you're sick and then you write about it, sometimes I want to die and then you do, sometimes I want stamps and then you want stamps, sometimes I want to cry on your shoulder like a little boy and then you want to cry on mine like a little girl. And sometimes and ten times and a thousand times and forever I want to be with you and you say the same thing. Enough, enough. (*LM*, 111)

Not having pressed Felice and Milena at the time of Kafka's death to surrender his letters for destruction or to destroy the letters themselves, Brod lost control over their subsequent fate. As the German army was entering Prague in 1939, Milena entrusted the letters in her possession to Willy Haas (1891–1973), a writer who was a friend of hers and had been a familiar of Kafka's circle. In 1952, Haas published them in Germany, arguing that Milena would have had no objection. The response of Milena's daughter to that farfetched assertion was that neither Milena nor Kafka would have ever consented. Accompanied by her husband and two children, Felice left Germany for Switzerland in 1931, and then emigrated to the United States in 1936, taking Kafka's letters with her. In 1955, five years before her death, she sold them to Schocken Books. Included in the sale were Kafka's letters to Grete Bloch (1892–1944), a friend whom she had introduced to Kafka, which Grete had given to her in 1935.

Although Kafka's fiction is austerely ahistorical, he did not write in a landscape as empty and uncharted as the wintry fields through which K., the hapless land surveyor, trudges on his way to Count Westwest's domain in *The Castle*. As Kafka gallantly pointed out to Felice, who had shown herself to be jealous of the attention he was devoting to his novel *Amerika*,

> Whatever happens I implore you, with hands raised in supplication, not to be jealous of my novel. If the people in it get wind of your jealousy, they will run away from me; as it is, I am holding on to them only by the ends of their sleeves. And imagine, if they run away from me I shall have to run after them, even as far as the underworld, where of course they really are at home. The novel is me, my stories are me—where, I ask you, would there be the tiniest place for jealousy? (*LF*, 138)

Anchored in Prague and Prague's German-speaking Jewish middle class, Kafka had the sensibility of a man of his place and time. Haas observed that

Kafka had certainly said it all, all that we had on the tips of our tongue and never said, never could say.... I cannot imagine how any man can understand him at all who was not born in Prague in the period 1880 to 1890.... Kafka seems to me to be...an Austrian, Jewish and Prague secret to which only we have the key.[2]

There is a good deal of exaggeration as well as an important grain of truth in Haas's elegant assertion, the truth being that even a modicum of knowledge about Kafka's life and his social context should enhance the experience of reading his work. Bohemia, Prague, and Kafka's family seem good places to start.

---

[2] W. Haas; *Die Literarische Welt*, Munich 1960, p. 33 f., quoted in Stölzl, Christoph, *Kafkas böses Böhmen: Zur Socialgeschichte eines Prager Juden* (Munich: edition + kritik, 1975), p. 16 f.

I

Life is merely terrible.

Franz Kafka, born in 1883, was the eldest child of Herrmann Kafka (1852–1932) and Julie, née Löwy (1856–1934). The family was Jewish. Kafka's two younger brothers died shortly after their birth. There were three younger sisters, born in Prague like Franz: Elli (1889–1941), Valli (1890–1942), and Ottla (1892–1943), Kafka's confidante and favorite. All three of them were murdered by Germans in concentration camps. Facing the pressure of Czech nationalist boycotts and violence directed at businesses owned by "Germans"—as the German-speaking population of Bohemia, whether gentile or Jewish, was called—Herrmann dropped first one "r" and then one "n" from his name, and became Herman. The point was to make his name less aggressively Teutonic.

"Prague doesn't let go," nineteen-year-old Kafka wrote to Oskar Pollak, his best friend at their pre-university secondary school. "This old crone has claws. One has to yield." (*L*, 5) At the time of Kafka's birth, the "old crone" was the third-most-important city of the Austro-Hungarian Empire, after Vienna and Budapest. It had been the capital of the ancient kingdom of Bohemia, of which the Habsburgs became the rulers in 1547 after Ferdinand I of that house, having brought to heel the Bohemian magnates, was recognized by the Bohemian diet as the sovereign of the land by hereditary right. The prize was rich: Ferdinand obtained, in addition to Bohemia proper, the important provinces of Moravia and Silesia. A measure of its value was that Prague became the capital of the Habsburg domains. In 1617, however, the capital moved to Vienna and, by the time Kafka was born, Bohemia was administered from Vienna as a Habsburg possession. It remained such until the end of World War I, when an independent Czech Republic was declared, consisting of Bohemia and Moravia. Adjacent Slovakia acceded to the republic within two days, whereupon the republic became Czechoslovakia. Bohemian Silesia had long since been lost to Prussia as a result of the War of Austrian Succession (1740–1748) and became part of Germany when the German states were unified in 1871. The Treaty of Versailles awarded part of Silesia to Poland.

The seventeenth century in Bohemia had been a period of brutally destructive internecine and religious wars. A steep economic decline ensued, and huge tracts of land belonging to old Czech nobility were expropriated and granted to foreign families that had provided mercenaries to the emperor. Bohemian Protestants were crushed and Roman Catholicism was proclaimed the state religion. As part of the repression, the Czech language was reduced to the status of a peasant dialect and German became the language of the administration and the upper and middle classes. Toward the end of the eighteenth century, however, a resurgent Czech nationalist movement, nourished by French revolutionary ideals, obtained reforms from Vienna that included the official recognition of Czech as a parallel language of instruction in schools and at the university in Prague. The fervor and bitterness of Czech nationalism increased in the nineteenth century, its rallying point and focus being hostility to all things German.

Bohemia and Moravia, as well as Austria itself and other Habsburg lands, had small but economically significant Jewish populations. The largest Jewish concentration in the empire by far was in Galicia, a Polish province until a partition of Poland awarded it to Austria. After the defeat of the Central Powers in 1918, most of Galicia reverted to the newly independent Polish Republic. Jews in Bohemia were subjected to a harsh regime: as elsewhere in Europe since the beginning of the Middle Ages, they were generally confined to ghettoes and suffered a multitude of legal restrictions and humiliations.

For instance, although Jews settled in the countryside usually did not live in ghettoes, they could not own or lease land. For years, Empress Maria Theresa made Jews pay a special tax for the privilege of being allowed to live in Bohemia. The French Revolution offered the prospect of an improved existence to European Jews. In 1789, the Declaration of the Rights of Man adopted by the revolutionary convention implicitly promised all men equality and religious freedom. The promise was redeemed for French Jews in 1791, when they were granted full-fledged citizenship. The wave of revolutions that convulsed continental Europe in 1848 resulted in Austria adopting the constitution of April 25, 1848, which granted free exercise of religion to all minorities in the Habsburg lands, Bohemia included; the constitution also abolished special taxes and other restrictions on Jews. A counterrevolution followed swiftly: the liberal but weak Emperor Ferdinand I abdicated and was followed on the throne by his much more conservative nephew, Emperor Franz Joseph. To the great rejoicing of Jews, however, Franz Joseph promulgated a new constitution in 1849: under it, Jews obtained important new rights, including the freedom to marry, to choose their place of residence, and to acquire real estate. The anti-Semitic response was violent throughout the empire, and especially in Bohemia, taking the form of agitation and anti-Jewish riots. Cutbacks in Jewish rights followed, but, in 1867, yet another new Habsburg constitution removed all legal disabilities applicable to Jews. The push to emancipate Jews was not a sign of imperial philo-Semitism—it was motivated by the government's calculation that Jewish entrepreneurial talents, if given full scope, would revive the stagnating economies of Austria and Bohemia. And in fact the "Bohemian Miracle," in which Jews played a large role, brought about rapid industrialization and development of commerce. The dark side of progress was manifested in the Vienna stock exchange crash of 1873 and the economic crisis of the 1880s, which combined to bring about a cataclysm on the scale of the Great Depression, and the liberals' election losses in 1879. Another by-product of rapid industrial growth was the destabilization of the Bohemian countryside, the blame for which fell on Jews.

There had previously been individual Jews in Austria-Hungary and the German states who had amassed large fortunes, and, having been being useful to their sovereigns, obtained the status of court Jews (*Hofjuden*) or protected Jews (*Schutzjuden*); this status shielded them from the ghetto system. They were the exceptions. For other Jews, the new rights were a hoped-for signal to crawl out from the medieval bog, take advantage of opportunities to live more freely, and to acquire a German education and German culture that would be their passport to middle-class status. For all the new optimism, however, Jews did not misinterpret the meaning of legal equality: it did not do away with de facto barriers erected by anti-Semitism and class sentiment. As a rule, the officer corps of the Habsburg army remained closed to Jews, as did teaching posts at the university and jobs in all but the lowest levels of the administration. However, until the closing decades of the nineteenth century, entry into the liberal professions was untrammeled in Austria-Hungary, and Jews became lawyers and doctors in numbers strikingly disproportionate to the percentage of the population they represented. A Jewish paradigm was established in Bohemia: Orthodox grandparents born in the first half of the century had eked out a living as tradespeople, peddlers, artisans, or innkeepers in villages and small towns, sometimes but not always in a ghetto; through ceaseless work their children prospered as merchants and gravitated to Prague or larger towns in search of greater opportunities and to escape the hatred directed at them by the Czech rural population. The second generation preserved the forms of Jewish religious practice, but Judaism no longer constituted the central fact of their lives. The grandchildren, even more detached from religious observance, entered one of the liberal professions or carried the family business to a higher level. Of course, not all children grasped the brass ring. Some became writers. A joke held that if one saw a Jew in a Prague café it was safe to assume that he was a writer.

The evolution of Kafka's family fit the pattern. By the time Kafka was born, his father, Herman, was established in Prague as the owner of a shop dealing in haberdashery and fashion accessories. However, as the fourth son of a ritual butcher in Wossek, a village of some hundred inhabitants in southern Bohemia, Herman lacked the education and polish that would have enabled him to join the higher ranks of the assimilated Jewish middle class. Kafka resented Herman's habit of rubbing the noses of his own more fortunate children in the dire poverty and hardships he had endured as the son of a butcher:

> It is unpleasant to listen to father talk with incessant insinuations about the good fortune of people today and the sufferings he had to endure in his youth. No one denies that for years, as a result of insufficient winter clothing, he had open sores on his legs, that he often went hungry, that when he was only ten he had to push a cart through the villages, even in winter and very early in the morning—but, and this

is something he will not understand, these facts taken together with the further fact that I have not gone through all this, by no means lead to the conclusion that I have been happier than he, that he may take pride in those sores on his legs which is something he assumes and asserts from that very beginning, that I cannot appreciate his past sufferings, and that, finally, just because I have not gone through the same sufferings I must be endlessly grateful to him.... How gladly I would listen if he would talk on about his youth and parents, but to hear all this in a boastful and quarrelsome tone is torment. Over and over again he claps his hands together: "Who can understand that today! What do the children know! No one has gone through that! Does a child understand that today!" (*D*, 154)

A Jew becomes a man at thirteen, after his bar mitzvah. From that point on, Herman had been on his own; he was put to work for a merchant in Pisek, a nearby town. Nonetheless, he had received enough instruction, presumably at the Jewish school in Wossek, to be able to read and write in Czech, which remained his primary language, as well as in German, which he spoke fluently. He also knew enough Hebrew to be able to find his way in the prayer book, and when at the synagogue he was called to pulpit to read from the Torah. At twenty he was drafted into the army. The ritual butcher had been a man of prodigious strength, reputed to be able to lift a sack of flour with his teeth. Herman took after his father. He thrived in military service and was promoted to the grade of corporal. Back in civilian life, he tried his luck again as a rural peddler but, like so many Jews, he found the political and social climate of Prague more tolerant. He settled there and one year later, in 1882, married Julie. His haberdashery and fashion accessories shop, which eventually evolved into a wholesale business, was opened with the financial assistance of the Löwy parents.

Julie's background was less rough. Assimilated and German-speaking, her parents were a generation ahead of Herman Kafka and his family in terms of social progress. Kafka composed a romanticized sketch of his maternal ancestors:

> In Hebrew my name is Amschel, like my mother's maternal grandfather, whom my mother, who was six years old when he died, can remember as a very pious and learned man with a long, white beard. She remembers how she had to take hold of the toes of the corpse and ask forgiveness for any offense she may have committed against her grandfather. She also remembers her grandfather's many books which lined the walls. He bathed in the river every day, even in winter, when he chopped a hole in the ice for his bath. My mother's mother died of typhus at an early age. From the time of this death her grandmother became melancholy, refused to eat, spoke with no one; once, a year after the death of her daughter, she went for a walk and did not return. Her body was found in the Elbe. An even more learned man than her grandfather was my mother's great-grandfather. Christians and Jews held him in equal honor. During a fire a miracle took place as a result of his piety: the flames jumped over and spared his house while the houses around it burned down. He had four sons, one was converted to Christianity and became a doctor. All but my mother's grandfather died young. He had one son, whom my mother knew as crazy uncle Nathan, and one daughter, my mother's mother. (D, 152–3)

Julie Kafka's father, Jakob Löwy, had been the owner of a drapery business in Podiebrad, a small historic town to the east of Prague. None of his sons having gone into the business, he sold it, moved to Prague, and established himself as a brewer sufficiently prosperous to live in Smetana House, one of the finest buildings in Prague. Jakob's brothers were also brewers or textile factory owners. At the time Herman married Julie, marriages among Jews were arranged; even if they weren't it was normal to marry only with the parents' approval. Uncultivated and poor, Herman was an odd choice as Julie's bridegroom. Perhaps her father and stepmother thought she was in danger of becoming an old maid; she was already twenty-six. It may also be that they recognized Herman's good qualities: his business sense, ambition, and desire to raise a family.

Kafka believed that there was an important dichotomy between the Kafka and Löwy sides of his family. In the *Letter to His Father*, which he had given to his mother for delivery to his father—a task she didn't perform—he told Herman that

as a father you have been too strong for me, particularly since my brothers died when they were small and my sisters came along only much later, so that I alone had to bear the brunt of it—and for that I was much too weak.

Compare the two of us: I, to put it in a very much abbreviated form a Löwy with a certain Kafka component which, however, is not set in motion by the Kafka will to life, business and conquests, but by a Löwyish spur that impels more secretly, more diffidently, and in another direction, and which often fails to work entirely. You on the other hand, a true Kafka in strength, health, appetite, loudness of voice, eloquence, self-satisfaction, worldly dominance, endurance, presence of mind, knowledge of human nature, a certain way of doing things on a grand scale, of course with all the defects and weaknesses that go with these advantages and into which your temperament and sometimes your hot temper drive you. (*S*, 117)

He saw his beloved youngest sister Ottla as an especially complicated case within the family:

Here was something like a kind of Löwy, equipped with the best Kafka weapons....the purest representation of the marriage between you and Mother, and of the forces it combined....On your side there was the tyranny of your nature, on her side the Löwy defiance, touchiness, sense of justice, restlessness and all that backed by the consciousness of the Kafka vigor. (*S*, 141)

There were many Kafka uncles and cousins. But it was the Löwy uncles, three of Julie's brothers and half-brothers, whose importance in Kafka's life and imagination was the greatest. Alfred (1852–1923), the "Madrid Uncle," a figure of some glamour in the eyes of his nephew, had risen to the position of director of a Spanish railroad company. At a crucial moment in 1907, he used his connections to help Kafka get his first job. Uncle Rudolf (1861–1922), who died a suicide, was the butt of Herman Kafka's jokes, the family fool who was content to rise no higher than the position of a bookkeeper at a brewery in a Prague suburb and remain a bachelor living with a father he couldn't bear. When it became evident that Kafka would not become a businessman and certainly wouldn't shine as a lawyer, Herman began to taunt him with his resemblance to Uncle Rudolf, a half-truth that Kafka, having recently plumbed the depth of his mother's lack of understanding for the complications of his personality, found it necessary to accept:

> When I look at my whole way of life going in a direction that is foreign and false to all my relatives and acquaintances, the apprehension arises, and my father expresses it, that I shall become a second Uncle Rudolf, the fool of the new generation of the family, the fool somewhat altered to meet the needs of a different period; but from now I'll be able to feel how my mother (whose opposition to this opinion grows continually weaker in the course of the years) sums up and enforces everything that speaks for me and against Uncle Rudolf, and that enters like a wedge between the conceptions entertained about the two of us. (*D*, 143–4)

In January 1922, Kafka suffered a grave nervous breakdown. It had become impossible for him to sleep or to stay awake or to endure life. "The clocks," he wrote, "are not in unison." (*D*, 398) His thoughts turned to his uncle Rudolf. The diary entry about the uncle sets out also a chilling self-portrait of the nephew at that time of extreme anxiety and depression:

> My resemblance to Uncle Rudolf, however, is even more disconcerting: both of us quiet (I less so), both dependent on our parents (I more so), at odds with our fathers, loved by our mothers (he in addition condemned to the horror of living with his father, though of course his father was likewise condemned to live with him), both of us shy, excessively modest (he more so), both regarded as noble, good men—there is nothing of these qualities in me and, so far as I know, very little in him (shyness, modesty, timidity

are accounted noble and good because they offer little resistance to other people's aggressive impulses)—both hypochondriacal at first, then really ill, both, for do-nothings, kept fairly well by the world (he, because he was less of a do-nothing, kept much more poorly, so far as it is possible to make a comparison now), both officials (he a better one), both living the most unvarying lives, with no trace of any development, young to the end of our days ('well-preserved' is a better expression), both on the verge of insanity; he far away from Jews, with tremendous courage, with tremendous vitality (by which one can measure the degree of the danger of insanity) escaped into the church where, so far as one could tell, his tendencies to madness were somewhat held in check, he himself had probably not been able for years to hold himself in check. One difference in his favor, or disfavor, was his having had less artistic talent than I, he could therefore have chosen a better path in life for himself in his youth, was not inwardly pulled apart, not even by ambition. Whether he had to contend (inwardly) with women, I do not know, a story by him that I read would indicate as much; when I was a child, moreover, they spoke of something of the sort....It isn't true that he was not good, I never found a trace of niggardliness, envy, hate, or greed in him; he was probably too unimportant a person to be able to help others. He was infinitely more innocent than I, there is no comparison. In single details he was my caricature, in essentials I am his. (*D*, 403–4)

The favorite uncle, however, was Siegfried (1867–1942), a country doctor in Triesch, a small town in Moravia. Kafka spent the 1907 August vacation with him. Writing to Brod, he claimed that he had been riding around on his motorcycle, drinking beer, herding cows and goats, raking hay in the meadows, and doing other assorted outdoor activities—including "hanging about the park until midnight with an irritatingly infatuated girl." (*L*, 25–6)

And it was Siegfried to whom, as we will see, the family turned at the time of Kafka's terminal illness. Like Uncle Rudolf, Siegfried committed suicide, in his case to avoid deportation to the Theresienstadt concentration camp.

Herman and Julie's small first apartment, where Kafka was born, was on Rathaussgasse, at the edge of Josefstadt, the old Jewish quarter that had been rebuilt as part of a program of urban renewal. To keep pace with its mounting prosperity, the family moved a number of times, into larger and more comfortable apartments within or near the confines of Prague's old town. The last move in Kafka's lifetime was in 1907, to the fine residential building known as Oppelt-Haus, on the corner of Alstädter Ring and Niklasstrasse. Besides the Kafkas, there lived in the apartment the family factotum, Marie Werner—always referred to as "Fräulein," she was a Jewish woman who spoke only Czech—the cook, two cats, and a canary. The family shop also moved in 1907, from Zeltnergasse 12 to larger quarters in the Kinsky Palace on the Altstädter Ring. Kafka's sisters shared a room. At the age of twenty-four, for the first time in his life, Kafka had a room of his own. However, it was a room more like a passageway, leading from the parents' bedroom to the living room and the communal bathroom.

Cohabitation with his family was, in any event, a torment for Kafka. He was squeamish and sensitive to noise, and in the family apartment the assault on his senses was constant. A diary entry in 1911 records his habitual distress:

I want to write, with a constant trembling on my forehead. I sit in my room, in the very headquarters of the uproar of the entire house. I hear all the doors close, because of their noise only the footsteps of those running between them are spared me, I hear even the slamming of the oven door in the kitchen. My father bursts through the door of my room and passes through in his dragging dressing-gown, the ashes are scraped out of the stove....Valli asks, shouting through the anteroom as though through a Paris street, whether Father's hat has been brushed yet, a hushing that claims to be friendly to me raises the shout of an answering voice....(*D*, 104)

The noise—and every other annoyance—might have been easier to bear if the father had not been its chief source, as during his ritual evening card game:

the clamor of card playing and later the usual conversation which Father carries on when he is well, loudly if not coherently. (*D*, 171)

Or when he made a fuss over Kafka's first nephew, little Felix, a case in which jealousy added to the torment:

It is now after lunch. Little Felix has just been conveyed in the governess' arms through my room into the bedroom; behind him comes my father, behind him my brother-in-law, behind him my sister. He has just been put down in my mother's bed, and now my father, from my room, is listening at the bedroom door in the hope that Felix will call him again, for he is the one Felix loves best of all. There, he has just called out "Dje-Dje," meaning Grandfather, and now my father, trembling with joy, opens the door several times, quickly pops his head through the door several times, and so entices the child to further Dje-Dje calls. (*LF*, 217)

"Since I was a child," Kafka reminded his father,

I was with you chiefly during meals, your teaching was to a large extent the teaching of proper behavior at table.... Because in accordance with your strong appetite and your particular predilection you ate everything fast, hot, and in big mouthfuls, the child had to hurry; there was a somber silence at table, interrupted by admonitions: "Eat first, talk afterward," or "faster, faster, faster," or "there you are, you see, I finished ages ago." Bones mustn't be cracked with the teeth, but you could. Vinegar must not be sipped noisily, but you could. The main thing was that the bread should be cut straight. But it didn't matter that you did it with a knife dripping with gravy. Care had to be taken that no scraps fall on the floor. In the end it was under your chair that were the most scraps. At table one wasn't allowed to do anything but eat, but you cleaned and cut your fingernails, sharpened pencils, cleaned your ears with a toothpick. (*S*, 124)

It is small wonder that Kafka became a convinced and proselytizing vegetarian—until the diet imposed on him as a means of combating tuberculosis made eating meat a necessity—or that he was addicted to "Fletcherizing," a nutrition fad invented and promoted by the British food faddist, Horace Fletcher (1849–1919), that called for chewing each mouthful thirty-two times.

Added to the disgust Kafka suffered at table was the horror of his parents' intimacy. In a letter written on July 7, 1913, a few weeks after having asked Felice for the first time to marry him, he wrote to her that "the very sight of those I spring from fills me with dismay." He went on to chronicle a visit to his family in the country:

> Yesterday by chance all of us—my parents, my sister and I—were obliged to walk for about an hour in the dark along a muddy road...in spite of all her efforts, my mother walked in so clumsy a fashion that she got her shoes, and undoubtedly her stockings and skirts as well, covered in dirt. Yet she was firmly convinced that she might have been in far worse mess, and on reaching home she asked me (in fun, of course) to acknowledge that fact by inspecting her shoes.... But believe me, I was quite unable to look down at them, because I was repelled, and not, as you might think, by the dirt. By then, however...I had come to feel some little affection, or rather admiration for my father for being able to put up with all this—with my mother and me, my sisters with their families in the country, and the confusion in their summer home where cotton wool is to be found lying among plates and a disgusting assortment of all kinds of objects on the beds; where one of my sisters, the middle one, is lying in bed with some slight throat infection, while her husband sits beside her and in fun as well as in earnest keeps calling her "My Precious" and "My All;" where the little boy, because he can't help himself while being played with, does his business on the floor in the middle of the room, where the two maids jostle each other in the performance of various duties, where my mother insists on waiting on everyone, where bread is spread with goose-drippings, which, if one is lucky, trickle down one's fingers.... It is not because they are relatives that I cannot bear to be in the same room with them, but merely because they

are people....I cannot live with people; I absolutely hate all my relatives, not because they are wicked, not because I don't think well of them...but simply because they are people with whom I live in close proximity....

He concluded by telling Felice that he

would be incomparably happier living in a desert, in a forest, on an island, rather than here in my room between my parents' bedroom and living room.... Felice, beware of thinking of life as commonplace, if by commonplace you mean monotonous, simple, petty. Life is merely terrible; I feel it as few others do. Often—and in my inmost self perhaps all the time— I doubt that I am a human being. (*LF*, 286–7)

Kafka could have decided not to visit his parents in the country. In Prague, the intimacy was impossible to avoid. During his second engagement to Felice, he copied an excerpt from a letter to her (apparently not sent) in his diary, responding to her not unreasonable comment that "it would not be the greatest of pleasures to sit at table at home with all your family." Without hiding his displeasure, he reminded her that he was linked to his parents and sisters by blood, and continued

Sometimes this bond of blood too is the target of my hatred; the sight of the double bed at home, the used sheets, the nightshirts carefully laid out, can exasperate me to the point of nausea, can turn me inside out; it is as if I had not been definitely born, were continually born anew into the world out of the stale life in that stale room, had consistently to seek confirmation of myself there, were indissolubly

joined with all that loathsomeness, in part even if
not entirely, at least it still clogs my feet which want
to run, they are still stuck in the original shapeless
pulp. (*D*, 371)

The salvo fired at Herman in the *Letter* was intended to
hurt. When Kafka gave it to Milena to read, he gave her due
warning: "as you read it understand all the lawyer's tricks: it
is a lawyer's letter." (*LM*, 63) The disclaimer, however, was a
lawyer's trick in itself, part false modesty and part rhetorical
device designed to win indulgence for his exaggerations by
an appearance of candor and preemptive self-criticism. It
was doubtless true that his father didn't mean to harm him,
but intentions count for little in the upbringing of children,
and the protestations scattered throughout the *Letter* that
his father was not responsible for the bad feelings between
them were disingenuous. Indeed, the most egregious of
the lawyer's tricks was to pretend that he loved his father.
Manifestly, he loathed him. In the way of sons who do
their duty without love, in July 1922, at a time when he
was himself a very sick man, Kafka traveled to Prague from
Planá, a village some sixty miles south from Prague, where
he had been convalescing under the care of Ottla, to be
at the bedside of Herman, who was recovering from an
operation. After the visit he told Brod that

[h]is affection for me diminished day by day (no, on
the second day it was at its peak, but then went down
steadily). And yesterday he could not get me out of
the room quickly enough, while he forced my mother
to stay…he has a scar on his back which in the past
made prolonged lying almost impossible for him;
in addition there is the difficulty of every change of
position for his heavy body, his irregular heart, the
bulky bandage, coughing, with its painful effect on

the incision, but above all his restless, unresourceful, and benighted mind....Yesterday he gestured with his hand as the nurse, whom I found wonderful, was leaving, a gesture that in his language can only mean "Bitch!" And this state of his (which perhaps only I can grasp in all its dreadfulness) will...go on for days....(*L*, 343)

Brod apparently replied that Felix Weltsch's father—Felix was Kafka's and Brod's friend—had mentioned Herman Kafka's speaking with "pride and flashing eyes" about his son Franz. Implacable, Kafka shrugged off the report:

In this case what is there to cause a father's eyes to light up? A son incapable of marriage, who could not pass on the family name; pensioned off at thirty-nine; occupied only with his weird kind of writing, the only goal of which is his own salvation or damnation; unloving; alienated from the Faith, so that a father cannot even expect him to say the prayers for the rest of his soul; consumptive, and as the father quite properly sees it, having got sick through his own fault...(*L*, 347)

In 1910, Kafka wrote out version after version of the following statement, each time expanding it:

When I think about it, I must say that my education has done me great harm in some respects. This reproach applies to a multitude of people—that is to say my parents, several relatives, individual visitors to our house, various writers, a certain particular cook who took me to school for a year, a crowd of teachers (whom I must press tightly together in my memory, otherwise one would drop out here and there—but since I have pressed them together so, the whole mass crumbles away bit by bit anyhow), a school inspector, slowly walking passersby; in short, this reproach twists through society like a dagger…(*D*, 15)

An objective assessment of Kafka's performance in elementary and secondary school, as reflected in his grades and recollection of friends, is more consistent with academic success than indifference and failure. But even without such evidence, Kafka's erudition and general culture would make it hard to believe that he had taken no interest in his studies.

After Kafka's final examination at the secondary school, Kafka's father ostensibly stood aside and allowed the son to choose his profession freely. The view Kafka took of the father's permissiveness—eighteen years later, when he wrote the *Letter*—was different, and characteristically unforgiving:

Ever since I could think, I have had such profound anxieties about asserting my spiritual and intellectual existence that I was indifferent to everything else… This was the state in which I was given the freedom of choice of career. But was I still capable of making any use of such a freedom? Had I still any confidence in my own capacity to achieve a real career? My valuation of myself was much more dependent on you than on anything else…your weight always dragged me down….Never shall I pass the first grade in grammar school, I thought, but I succeeded, I even got a prize; but I shall certainly not pass the entrance exam for the Gymnasium [secondary school], but I succeeded; but now I shall certainly fail in the first year at the Gymnasium; no I did not fail and I went on succeeding and succeeding....Lessons, and not only lessons, but everything around me, interested me as much, at that decisive age, as an embezzling bank clerk, still holding his job and trembling at the thought of discovery, is interested in the petty ongoing business of the bank....So it went up to the final examinations in the gymnasium which I really passed only through cheating....So there was actually no such thing for me as freedom to choose my career for I knew: compared to the main thing everything would be exactly as much a matter of indifference to me as all the subjects taught at school, and so it was a matter of finding a profession that would let me indulge this indifference without injuring my vanity too much. Law was the obvious choice. Little contrary attempts on the part of vanity, of senseless hope, such as a fortnight's study of chemistry, or six months' German studies, only reinforced that fundamental conviction. So I studied law. This meant that in the few months before the exams, and in a way that told severely on my nerves, I was positively living, in an intellectual sense, on sawdust, which had moreover been chewed for me in thousands of other people's mouths. (S, 151–4)

The central fact is that Kafka's plan for his career had quickly boiled down to finding a dignified and secure occupation that would leave him enough time for his writing, and not be so arduous as to drain him of intellectual and psychic energy. His initial choice of German letters is easily understood, but he did not like the philological approach taken at the university in Prague. Besides, as a Jew he could not expect the study of literature to lead to a university position with a livable wage. Chemistry was considered a potentially promising field of studies: it could enable even a Jew to find desirable employment in a private firm. Unfortunately,

Kafka found that he had no aptitude for science. That circumstance also foreclosed medicine, the other traditional solution for Jews who did not go into business or become lawyers. Business—the family business—too was out of the question. The result of his father's method of upbringing, Kafka wrote in the *Letter*, "was that I fled everything that even remotely reminded me of you." (*S*, 135) That left the law, the path Kafka chose, although he had no intention of becoming a practicing lawyer. It was usual for law graduates with career objectives so limited and unambitious to set their sights on government service, but for a Jew entry into the Austrian administration was still all but impossible, except at the lowest level.

Kafka's academic performance during the five years of law studies was undistinguished. Cramming for exams was the occasion of a first breakdown, probably more nervous than physical, that led him in July 1905 to seek a rest cure at a sanatorium in Zuckmantel, in Austrian Silesia. After more cramming during the academic year 1905–6, Kafka squeaked through the qualifying examinations, and on June 16, 1906 was awarded the degree of doctor of law. Having already spent two months as an unpaid clerk in the office of a Prague lawyer, he served as a trainee during the academic year 1906–7 at the Prague court, first in the civil and then in the criminal section. Such training was a prerequisite only for entry into the Austrian administration, and therefore unnecessary in Kafka's case. However, it turned out to be a boon, giving Kafka access to material he drew on when he wrote about the court in *The Trial*. He would acquire additional valuable material— an insider's experience with the functioning of the state bureaucracy—working for his eventual lifetime employer, a semigovernmental insurer, from the summer of 1908 until the summer of 1922, and put it to use in *The Castle*, as well as in *The Trial*.

The search for an appropriate position in the private sector was complicated by Kafka's desire to be on the "single shift" system, in force in the state bureaucracy and only a handful of private enterprises. That system—office hours from eight or nine in the morning until two or three in the afternoon, at which point the workday ended—was in Kafka's opinion essential if he was to be able to write during a part of the afternoon and be sufficiently fresh to write in the evening. His lackluster record as a doctoral candidate proved to be a stumbling block. Finally, Uncle Alfred, the "Madrid uncle," obtained for him through the intercession of a Prague acquaintance a temporary position with the Prague office of a Trieste insurance company, Assicurazioni Generali. Kafka took it gratefully, thinking that after the training period he might be sent to one of the company's other foreign offices. His old dream, that the Madrid uncle would help him break away from his family and Prague and escape the life of mediocrity that stretched ahead, would have thus come true. He confided to Hedwig Weiler, the "irritatingly infatuated girl" encountered in Triesch:

> I am at the Assicurazioni Generali and have some hopes of some day sitting in chairs in faraway countries, looking out of the office windows at fields of sugar cane or Mohammedan cemeteries…(*L*, 35)

But Assicurazioni was not only on the double shift—office hours were from eight in the morning until six in the evening, with two hours off for lunch—but the other work conditions were singularly harsh as well. Overtime was mandatory and frequently demanded, supervisors were in the habit of brutalizing junior employees, the pay was low, and Kafka would have been entitled to two weeks of vacation only after he had completed two years on the job. He saw no possibility of finding time to write in these circumstances; indeed it does not appear that he wrote anything while he worked at Assicurazioni. However, his experience there may have contributed to the description in *Amerika* of Uncle Jacob's business headquarters, with its maddening noise and robotic telephone operators. Assicurazioni's other gift to Kafka readers is its examining physicians' report on his physical condition in 1907, which has survived in the insurance company's files. He weighed 61 kilograms (133 pounds) and measured 1.82 meters (not quite six feet). The average Czech was only five foot five to five foot six, and the average Czech Jew five foot to five foot one.[3] The doctor found him relatively weak and delicate, but overall in good health. Kafka's own opinion was less favorable. A diary entry in 1911 sets the tone of incessant complaints that continued until the fall of 1917, when tuberculosis made hypochondria superfluous:

> It is certain that a major obstacle to my progress is my physical condition. Nothing can be accomplished with such a body. I shall have to get used to its perpetual balking. As a result of the last few nights spent in wild dreams but with scarcely a few snatches of sleep, I was so incoherent this morning, I felt nothing but my forehead, saw a half-way bearable condition only far beyond my present one, and in sheer readiness to die would have been glad simply to have curled up on the cement floor of the corridor with the documents in my hand. My body is too long for its weakness, it hasn't the least bit of fat to engender a blessed warmth, to preserve an inner fire, no fat on which the spirit could occasionally nourish itself beyond its daily need

---

3 Gilman, Sander L. *Franz Kafka: The Jewish Patient* (New York: Routledge, 1995), p. 41.

without damage to the whole. How shall the weak
heart that lately has troubled me so often be able to
pound the blood through all the length of these legs?
It would be labor enough to the knees, and from there
it can only spill with a senile strength into the cold
lower parts of my body. (*D*, 124–5)

In reality, having overcome the humiliations of the
boyhood visits to the swimming school with his father,
his scrawny body contrasting with Herman's muscles and
bulk, he had become a strong and enthusiastic swimmer.
In August 1911, he wrote in his diary:

The time which has just gone by in which I haven't
written a word has been so important for me because I
have stopped being ashamed of my body in the swimming schools in Prague, Königssaal, and Czernoshitz.
(*D*, 50)

He had turned also into an oarsman who enjoyed taking a skiff
out on the Moldau, the river that flows through Prague, and
an inveterate walker. When the occasion presented itself, he
rode on horseback or on a motorcycle and played tennis.

During the year at Assicurazioni, Kafka was an eager
participant in Prague nightlife. Possibly he realized that
he was unable to write in the evening, and might as well
put his time to another use. In addition to movies and
operettas, Prague by night offered many diversions that
weren't likely to overtax the mind of an office worker who
had put in ten or more hours at work. No fewer than thirty-
five brothels operated in the city in 1905. By 1916, that
number was reduced to twenty-three, with a total of about
one hundred inmates. There were also some five hundred
prostitutes plying the streets, and as many as six thousand
more clandestine sex workers. Kafka frequented the better

brothels. He also liked cabarets and all-night cafés, where waitresses combined serving guests wine until closing time with other, more personal, services offered afterward. His favorite waitress was one Hansi; a photograph taken with her has survived. Kafka surely thought of her and her colleagues when he created Brunelda, the obese praying mantis of *Amerika*; the cabaret waitress whom Joseph K. visits once a week, the sexually aggressive Leni, and the washerwoman in *The Trial*; and Frieda and Pepi in *The Castle*.

Kafka's unhappiness at Assicurazioni Generali was such that within months he began to look for another position. Once again, he found someone willing to use influence on his behalf. The father of Ewald Príbram, one of Kafka's gymnasium and university friends (in 1940, he committed suicide to escape Nazi arrest), was Dr. Otto Príbram, the president of the *Arbeiter-Unfall-Versicherungs Anstalt* (the Workers' Accident Insurance Institute, a semi-governmental institution charged with insuring workers against industrial accidents and conducting inspections of factories to investigate compliance with safety standards). Dr. Príbram's position was an anomaly. In principle, the Institute was closed to Jews, and he was a Jew who apparently had not converted. Prevailed upon by his son, he arranged for Kafka to be hired on July 30, 1908, as a probationary employee in the industrial insurance division, making him the Institute's second Jewish employee.

The other was Dr. Siegmund Fleischmann, likewise an unconverted Jew. No other Jew was hired in Kafka's lifetime. His sensitivity to the ambient anti-Semitism is illustrated by his reply, after nine years on the job, to a request of his friend, Oskar Baum, for assistance with the case of a Jewish veteran who had lost his sight as a result of war injuries. Baum had himself been blinded as a young boy in a street altercation with gentile schoolboys who attacked him and his friends. Kafka was by then on one of his many medical leaves, and wrote to Baum that he couldn't take up the matter with his director, Dr. Robert Marschner, contacts with whom, by reason of Kafka's illness, had been reduced to the director's acting "only as a kind Providence, endlessly forbearing and patient and paying the bill." But he could refer Baum to the head of the relevant office, Dr. Fleischmann, "the first, myself the second and last crumbling Jew of the organization," who would be favorably disposed toward the veteran. (*L*, 161) Some weeks later, Brod asked Kafka to help Georg Langer, an Orthodox Jew, whom they both knew—and from whom they would soon be taking Hebrew lessons—get a job at the Institute. Kafka refused with atypical callousness:

> I cannot help Langer in this way. The Institute is closed to Jews. It would not amuse me to put such a fearful imposition upon the director—for that is what a prospective employee's request to be excused from work on Saturday would be. There is no explaining how two Jews, with the help of the third Jew [Dr. Príbram] got in, and it won't happen again. But perhaps there is some place for Langer in our shop, if that can be justified to Father…But Langer is strong; why doesn't he hire himself out to some Jewish tenant farmer? (*L*, 165)

The working conditions at the Institute were a considerable improvement over what Kafka had experienced at Assicurazioni, the much-desired single-shift system at the Institute being of crucial importance. It enabled Kafka to claim that he had adopted the routine he described to Felice in one of his first letters to her:

> from eight to two or 2:30 in the office, then lunch till three or 3:30, after that sleep in bed (usually only

attempts...) until 7:30, then ten minutes of exercises, naked at the open window, then an hour's walk—alone, with Max, or with another friend, then dinner with my family (I have three sisters, one married, one engaged; the single one, without prejudicing my affection for the others, is easily my favorite); then at 10:30 (but often not till 11:00) I sit down to write, and I go on, depending on my strength, inclination, and luck, until one, two, or three o'clock, once even till six in the morning. Then again exercises, as above, but of course avoiding all exertions, a wash, and then, usually with a slight pain in my heart and twitching stomach muscles, to bed. Then every imaginable effort to go to sleep... thus the night consists of two parts: one wakeful, the other sleepless...So it is hardly surprising if at the office the next morning, I only just manage to start work with what little strength is left. (*LF*, 22)

Anyone writing fiction who is accustomed to balancing the requirements of his day job and his writing is likely to be struck by how little time was reserved for writing in this well-ordered and depressingly petit bourgeois day. Even those few hours would be regularly reduced by the time devoted to correspondence with Felice, and, to a smaller extent, the diary and letters to friends. Usually, Kafka's letters were long, even if their subject matter was banal, and the questions he asked could have been put in the course of a quick phone call—if telephones had been in general use at the time, and Kafka had not had an aversion to telephone conversations. When Felice wrote to him a year later arguing that a more rational organization of his day might be possible, he bristled. The rites according to which he organized his time were not to be tinkered with by others, not even the woman he claimed to love:

The present way is the only possible one; if I can't bear it, so much the worse; but I will bear it somehow. One to two hours for writing is not enough (apart from the fact that you have not allocated any time for writing to you); ten hours would be perfect, but since perfection cannot be achieved one must at least come as close to it as possible, and not give a thought to sparing oneself. (*LF*, 180)

Fourteen months later, his employment by the Institute was made permanent, and in April 1910 he was promoted to the position of *Konzipist*, a "drafting clerk." Other promotions followed: he became a vice secretary of the Institute in 1913, secretary in 1920, and in 1922, shortly before he was pensioned off for medical reasons, senior secretary. These were responsible positions that commanded respect at an institution that was itself of considerable importance. Kafka's constant complaints about his work at the Institute notwithstanding, he was a valued official. His talents were recognized and he was able to apply them to tasks ranging from the composition of the Institute's annual reports and technical articles all the way to accident-prevention techniques. A notable achievement, resulting from his grasp of production methods, was his offer of suggestions for the improvement of safety features of planing machines used in the lumber industry. They were implemented and resulted in the prevention of countless injuries. He was liked and esteemed by his colleagues and treated with remarkable understanding by his superiors during the five years of the illness that permitted him to attend to his duties only sporadically. The promotions given him during a time when he was on sick leave more often than at the office are particularly striking. His relationship with Eugen Pfohl, his immediate superior until 1917, to whom he always referred in his letters as the Chief, was especially close; he had become Pfohl's right hand. Max Brod claimed that Kafka didn't have a single enemy at the Institute, that he had been the "office baby." (*B*, 82) Similarly, Gustav Janouch (1903–68), the son of one of Kafka's colleagues at the Institute, recalled in his memoir about contacts with Kafka his father's saying "Kafka personifies patience and kindness. I cannot remember an occasion when there was trouble in the institution on his account."(*J*, 63)

Everything had gone according to Kafka's plan, however unenthusiastically adopted: he held a secure position in a single-shift institution and had duties that, however demanding, he was apparently able to put out of his mind when he left the office—but the plan didn't work. In February 1911, he attempted to make his dilemma clear to Pfohl, in a draft letter that may not have been finished or sent:

> When I wanted to get out of bed this morning I collapsed. This has a simple cause, I am completely overworked. Not by the office but by my other work. The office has an innocent share in it only to the extent that, if I did not have to go there, I could live calmly for my own work and should not have to waste these six hours a day which have tormented me to a degree that you cannot imagine, especially on Friday and Saturday, because I was full of my own things… for me it is a horrible double life from which there is probably no escape but insanity. I write this in the good light of the morning and would certainly not write it if it were not so true and if I did not love you like a son. (*D*, 37–8)

The mention of "my things" was but a hint of the plenitude of powers he felt. Later that year, after a night of insomnia, which he had fought by lying on his back with his arms crossed, so as to make himself "as heavy as possible, which I consider good for falling asleep," he wrote:

> In the evening and in the morning my consciousness of the creative abilities in me is more than I can encompass. I feel shaken to the core of my being and can get out of myself whatever I desire. (*D*, 62)

The work for the Institute, he was convinced, interfered with that all-important process of mining his material and giving his full measure as a writer. A diary entry made shortly thereafter recorded his frustration:

> The bitterness I felt yesterday evening when Max read aloud my little motor-car story at Baum's. [Description of a traffic accident in Paris, *D*, 462–5.]...The disordered sentences of this story with holes into which one can stick both hands; one sentence sounds high, one sentence sounds low...one sentence rubs against another like the tongue against a hollow or false tooth, one sentence comes marching up with so rough a start that the whole story falls into sulky amazement. I explain it to myself by saying that I have too little time and quiet to draw out of me all the possibilities of my talent. For that reason it is only disconnected starts that always make an appearance....If I were ever able to write something large and whole, well-shaped from the beginning to end, then in the end the story would never be able to detach itself from me and it would be possible for me calmly and with open eyes, as a blood relation of a healthy story, to hear it read, but as it is every little piece of the story runs around homeless and drives me away from it in the opposite direction. (*D*, 104–5)

At the same time, he understood the danger and crippling effect on him of single-minded devotion to his art. After a New Year's Eve party to welcome 1912, which left him feeling estranged from Brod, he wrote:

> It is easy to recognize a concentration in me of all my forces on writing. When it became clear in my organism that writing was the most productive direction for my being to take, everything rushed in that direction and left empty all those abilities which were directed toward the joys of sex, eating, drinking, philosophical reflection, and above all music. This was necessary because the totality of my strengths was so light that only collectively could they even halfway serve the purpose of writing. (*D*, 163)

Awareness of the perilous dilemma to which writing exposed him never left Kafka, not even when he was surest of his great talent, as after the extraordinarily productive three months when he wrote "The Judgment," "The Stoker," and *The Metamorphosis*, and was working on the second version of *Amerika*, of which "The Stoker" was the first chapter:

> The tremendous world I have inside my head, but how to free myself and free it without being torn to pieces. And a thousand times rather be torn to pieces than retain it in me or bury it. That, indeed, is why I am here, that is quite clear to me. (*D*, 222)

As he explained to Felice, over and over, the need to write trumped all other considerations and desires.

So long as Kafka was working productively on his fiction, he could take in his stride the demands of his work for the Institute. Thus, in November 1912, he complained to Felice about having been obliged to go on a business trip and interrupt work on *The Metamorphosis*, but the tone was almost breezy:

> Well today, dearest, I shall have to put aside my story, I have worked on it today nowhere near as much as yesterday, and on account of that maddening trip to Kratzau I will have to let it wait for a day or two. This grieves me, but I hope the story won't suffer too much, though I shall need another three–four evenings to finish it. By "won't suffer too much," I mean that my story, alas, has been harmed enough through my method of working. This kind of story should be written with no more than one interruption, in two ten-hour sessions; then it would have its natural spontaneous flow, as it had in my head last Sunday. But I haven't got twice ten hours at my disposal. So one has to try to do the best one can, since the very best has been denied to one. (*LF*, 64)

Noise and the comings and goings in the family apartment were another major obstacle to creation. It had begun to seem to him that marriage to Felice would be one as well. He wrote in his diary in July 1913: "I must be alone a great deal," and "[W]hat I have accomplished was only the result of being alone." (*D*, 225) A page later, he got right to the point: "Alone, I could perhaps some day really give up my job. Married, it will never be possible." (*D*, 226) That was in all probability a realistic assessment, but Felice held out hope that he would fulfill his destiny as a man through marriage and perhaps fatherhood, both of which he was convinced he desired but also dreaded: "The connection with F. will give my existence more strength to resist." (*D*, 225)

But the absolute imperative was writing. In August 1913, he explained to Felice: "I have no literary interests, but am made of literature, I am nothing else and cannot be anything else." (*LF*, 304) How little Felice understood this imperative and the nonnegotiable conditions with which it was surrounded may be seen from her remarkably foolish but surely well-meant offer. She would sit quietly at his side while he wrote. Kafka's response was a bolt from Olympus:

> In that case I could not write at all. For writing means revealing oneself to excess: that utmost self-revelation and surrender, in which a human being, when involved with others, would feel he was losing himself, and from which therefore he will always shrink as long as he is in his right mind...even that degree of self-revelation and surrender is not enough for writing. This is why one can never be alone enough when one writes, why there can never be enough silence around one when one writes, why even night is not night enough. That is why there is never enough time at one's disposal, for the roads are long and it is easy to go astray...I have often thought that the best mode of life for me would be to sit in the innermost room of a spacious locked cellar with my writing things and a lamp.... And how I would write! From what depths I would drag it up! Without effort! For extreme concentration knows no effort. (*LF*, 155–6)

He knew, of course, that anyone looking in from the outside might see the obvious solution: he should quit the job at the Institute, move out of his parents' apartment, and take a chance on being able to support himself with his pen. That solution, however, even if otherwise acceptable, and it wasn't, was inconsistent with the course he was on, which was to marry Felice. He had perfected a riposte to any such suggestion, and, in a letter to Felice's father that he was drafting in August 1913, soon after he had asked Felice to marry him, he resorted to it preemptively:

> My job is unbearable to me because it conflicts with my only desire and my only calling, which is literature. Since I am nothing but literature and can and want to be nothing else, my job will never take possession of me, it may however, shatter me completely, and this is by no means a remote possibility. Nervous states of the worst sort control me without pause, and this year of worry and torment about my and your daughter's future has revealed to me my full inability to resist. You might ask why I do not give up this job and—I have no money—do not try to support myself by literary work. To this I can make only the reasonable reply that I haven't the strength for it, and that, as far as I can see, I shall instead be destroyed by this job, and destroyed quickly. (*D*, 230)

It isn't known whether Kafka actually sent this letter to Herr Bauer.

Of course, Kafka's situation was by no means unusual. To take but two examples in his own circle of closest friends, Brod, who had never doubted that his true calling was to be a writer, and was already a published author, worked for the postal service; Felix Weltsch (1884–1964), who edited the Prague Jewish weekly *Selbstwehr*, and would become a noted philosopher, worked for the university library. But Kafka differed from his prolific and normally functioning friends. Inspiration—the voice he needed to hear in order to write—did not come to him reliably; he was fragile, and as Brod and perhaps others had come to understand, he was a genius. A genius, moreover, who had laid down for himself the rule that "[b]readwinning and the art of writing must be kept absolutely apart." (*B*, 79) If there was to be a solution it had to be one that recognized Kafka's special needs, limitations, and constraints. Writing to Felice Bauer, shortly after Kafka's mother had become aware of her correspondence with Franz, Brod told her:

> If his parents love him so much, why don't they give him 30,000 Gulden as they would to a daughter, so that he could leave the office, go off to some cheap little place on the Riviera to create those works that God, using Franz's brain, wishes the world to have.—So long as Franz is not in a position to do this, he will never be entirely happy. His whole disposition cries out for a peaceful, trouble-free existence dedicated to writing. (*LF*, 57)

However, as Brod knew, even if one assumed that it was at the time within Herman's financial means to give his son a dowry, it was inconceivable that he could be persuaded to do so. Herman would have had to be a radically different kind of man: one who set a high value on literature and believed in his son's ability. Instead, he was a loud, anti-intellectual bully who "put special trust in bringing up children by means of irony," and had no use for his son's writing. (*S*, 128) Franz was far more realistic than Brod about his own ability to allow, let alone force, his parents to support him. In the fall of 1911, he consoled himself, "although it is actually the opposite of consoling," by writing down an autobiographical remark of George Bernard Shaw's. Shaw, who had given up a position as a miserably underpaid apprentice in an office in Dublin, and had gone off to London, disregarding his family's straitened circumstances, did not throw himself into the struggle for a livelihood. He found another way: "I threw my mother in and let her support me. I was no support for my old father; on the contrary, I hung on to his coattails." What Shaw had done, Kafka recognized, was beyond his own strength; he "was cowardly and miserable enough to follow Shaw only to the extent of having read the passage to my parents." (*D*, 90–1) Evidently, they were unimpressed.

The other horn of the dilemma, to which one is forced time and again to return, was Kafka's unwillingness or inability to take risks. Misunderstood sons routinely leave the homes of their philistine parents, especially once they have secured, as Kafka had, a position that affords them a reasonable level of financial independence. Impoverished writers quit steady jobs in order to follow the Muse, braving penury and worse. That was not Kafka's way. He didn't resign from the Insurance Institute until its own physician declared him unfit for duty. When he left Prague in September of 1923 for Berlin it was as a desperately ill man, and even then he maintained the fiction that it was only a temporary move and he would soon return. In Brod's recollection, Herman Kafka was a decent, businesslike man. Perhaps he was, but Herman's son saw his father as his tormentor, forever a giant of a man who, when Kafka was a child and whimpered at night for water "probably partly to be annoying, partly to amuse myself," took him out of bed, set him on the *pavlatche* (a sort of balcony running along the circumference of the inner courtyard of old buildings in Prague), shut the door, and left him there in his nightshirt. This was an expedient, Kafka wrote, that made him quite obedient afterward, "but it did me inner harm."(*S*, 119)

In any event, Brod's wish that the father give Kafka enough money to make it possible for him to work exclusively on his fiction was probably misguided. Kafka's failure to make even an attempt to break out of the twin prisons of the

Institute and his room at the family apartment may have been nothing less than the choice of the way of life that paradoxically best suited him.

It is rare that writers of fiction sit behind their desks, actually writing, for more than a few hours a day. Had Kafka been able to use his time efficiently, the work schedule at the Institute would have left him with enough free time for writing. As he recognized, the truth was that he wasted time. Complete freedom—relief from the constraints imposed by the Institute and myriad annoyances from which he suffered at home—and the ability to stare all day at the blank page might well have been unbearable for him. Every writer's worst nightmare, one especially terrifying for a writer whose talent was, as he believed, to portray his "dreamlike inner life," is to be incapable of beginning or completing a work. (*D*, 302) Having the Institute and the conditions at his parents' apartment to blame for the long fallow periods when he couldn't write gave Kafka cover: it enabled him to preserve some of his self-esteem. The need to preserve it was real; in comparison with his friends he was a laggard. For example, Max Brod had been publishing short stories, poems, and essays since the age of twenty. His first novel and fourth book, *Schloss Nornepygge*, hailed by German critics as a masterpiece of expressionism, appeared in 1908, when he was twenty-four—the year in which, through Brod's intercession and with his encouragement, Kafka published in the bimonthly periodical *Hyperion* his first slim collection of eight short prose pieces. Although another close friend, Oskar Baum (1883–1941), was blind, a collection of his short stories was also published that year; his very successful novel, *Das Leben in Dunkeln* [Life in Darkness], came one year later. Franz Werfel (1890–1945) was seven years younger than Kafka, but he too was precocious. At the age of twenty-two he published a collection of poems that was greeted with critical acclaim.

Feeling that he was stuck in the family apartment and at the Institute job like a fly on flypaper, knowing that he hadn't Werfel's glittering facility, Kafka couldn't help being ambivalent about him. In 1911 he wrote in his diary:

> I hate Werfel, not because I envy him, but I envy him too. He is healthy, young and rich, everything that I am not. Besides, gifted with a sense of music, he has done very good work early and easily, he has the happiest life behind him and before him, I work with weights I cannot get rid of, and I am entirely shut off from music. (*D*, 141)

He expressed similar feelings that year about Oskar Baum, whose play, *Konkurrenz* [Competition], had been given a public reading in Prague at the end of October of that year and would be published shortly afterward. After the performance, Kafka wrote in his diary that it was excellent but depressed him. (*D*, 97) A few days later, he returned to the subject of the play:

> Envy of the apparent success of Baum whom I like so much. With this, the feeling of having in the middle of my body a ball of wool that quickly winds itself up, its innumerable threads pulling from the surface of my body to itself. (*D*, 103)

Fortunately, his good nature and growing confidence in his own powers didn't allow envy or resentment to predominate. Thus, one year later, he found himself able to tell Felice, with only a hint of resentment, that:

> Werfel is really miraculous; when I read his book... for the first time (I had heard him recite poetry before that), I thought I was going off my head with

enthusiasm....What's more, he has already got his reward; he lives in Leipzig in blissful conditions, he is an editor at Rowohlt...and at the age of 24 has complete freedom to live and write. (*LF*, 102)

But that was not all: Kafka also had before his eyes his friends' ability to face and overcome great adversity. As a boy, Brod had suffered from scoliosis, which was treated when he was an adolescent by a rigid corrective corset that he was obliged to wear constantly. For years he had been in constant pain. Nevertheless, he had turned into a self-sufficient and vigorous man who was married and soon would also have a turbulent emotional life outside his marriage. The comparison with the blind Oskar Baum, who supported himself as an organist and had, in addition, become a successful writer, and had also married and lived an apparently normal life, must have been even more humbling. Kafka's feeling that he had fallen short persisted. In April 1921, in a letter to Brod written from the sanatorium in Matliary, Kafka allowed his bitterness to spill over while expressing admiration for the way his friends managed their careers: "Myself? When the news about you, Felix [Weltsch], and Oskar is all set down, and I compare myself with the three of you, it seems to me that I am wandering like a child in the forests of maturity." (*L*, 270)

Even when his work went well, Kafka felt the need for excuses, some of them perennial favorites, to justify not having done better or more. Thus, on the last day of 1914, at age of thirty-one, he took stock of his production as follows:

Have been working since August, in general not little nor badly, yet neither in the first nor in the second respect to the limit of my ability, as I should have done, especially as there is every indication (insomnia, headaches, weak heart) that my ability won't last much longer. Worked on, but did not finish: The Trial, "Memoirs of the Kalda Railway," "The Village Schoolmaster," "The Assistant Attorney," and the beginnings of various little things. Finished only: In the Penal Colony and a chapter of Der Verschollene [Amerika] both during the two-week holiday. I don't know why I am drawing up this summary. It's not at all like me. (*D*, 324)

In reality, to have done as much was a remarkable achievement, even if both novels were ultimately abandoned.

Kafka complained again a few days later:

Great desire to begin another story; didn't yield to it. It is all pointless. If I can't pursue the stories through the nights they break away and disappear, as with the "Assistant Attorney" [a story that has been lost] now. And tomorrow I go to the factory, perhaps I shall have to go there every afternoon after P. [Peppa, Kafka's brother-in-law] reports for duty. With that, every thing is at an end. The thought of the [asbestos factory in which the Kafka family had an investment] is my perpetual Day of Atonement. (*D*, 324–5)

And ten days later, he resolved to order his time better:

Realized that I have by no means made satisfactory use of the time since August. My constant attempts, by sleeping a great deal in the afternoon, to make it possible for myself to continue working late into the night were absurd; after the first two weeks I could already see that my nerves would not permit me to go to bed after one o'clock, for then I can no longer fall asleep at all, the next day is insupportable and I destroy myself. I lay down too long in the afternoon,

> though I seldom worked later than one o'clock at
> night, and always began about eleven o'clock at the
> earliest. That was a mistake. I must begin at eight
> or nine o'clock; the night is certainly the best time
> (holiday!), but beyond my reach. (*D*, 325)

The dream that he might succeed in completing and selling
a substantial piece of work and become financially able to
move to Berlin did not leave Kafka, but its realization was
to become infinitely more difficult for practical reasons: the
outbreak of World War I and, after August 1917, knowledge
that he had tuberculosis.

One cannot be sure that Kafka realized how much he had
missed in the great world that lay beyond Prague, the various
sanatoria he had frequented, and the little he had seen of
Berlin and Vienna. His early holiday travels with Brod in
1911 and 1912 are recorded in Kafka's *Travel Diaries*. (*D*,
427–87) They visited Friedland and Reichenberg in northern
Bohemia in the early spring of 1911, and Switzerland,
northern Italy, and Paris in the summer of that year. In July
1912, they went to Weimar. Reading the *Travel Diaries*, one
knows at once that they are the work of a real writer with
an ability to seize and put down on paper details that make
the scene he is describing lively, disturbing, and memorable.
This is true especially of the descriptions of visits to brothels
in Milan and Paris. Thus, in Milan:

> The girls spoke their French like virgins. . . . A girl with
> a belly that had undoubtedly spread shamelessly over
> and between her outspread legs under her transparent
> dress while she had been sitting down; but when
> she stood up it was pulled in and the body at last
> looked something like what a girl's body should be.
> (*D*, 444)

And in Paris:

> The female concierge who rang her electric bell...the
> two respectable-looking women upstairs (why two?)
> who received us; the light switched on in the adjoining
> room in the darkness or semi-darkness of which were
> sitting the unengaged girls; the three quarter circle
> (we made it a full circle) in which they stood around
> us, drawn up in postures calculated to reveal them
> to best advantage; the long stride with which the girl
> who had been chosen came forward; the grasp with
> which the madam urged me on, while I felt myself
> impelled toward the exit. (*D*, 459)

There are also comments on the obligatory sightseeing in the cathedral in Milan, and in Paris at the Louvre and the Opéra-Comique.

But one cannot help being struck by the lack of sophistication of this pair of intellectuals and writers. Their itinerary and activities are those of banal tourists. Because of their age—Brod was thirty and Kafka was twenty-nine—and the limitations of their Prague milieu, it isn't surprising that they had no introductions to other writers or scholars, but one might expect a mention of their having wished to meet such people, or at least to gawk at them, and some awareness of the new forms of literature, painting, sculpture, and music that were taking root and blossoming in Paris.

Something akin to provincialism—a sense that Kafka was confined in a backwater—marks the diaries and correspondence. His reading was very broad, but by and large it stopped at the end of the nineteenth century. Among the masters who continued to be active in the early years of the twentieth century and were exerting powerful influence over younger writers, he was very much aware of August Strindberg (1849–1912) and Frank Wedekind

(1864–1918), and read and admired their plays. He wrote
to Brod that Thomas Mann (1875–1955) "is one of the
writers whose work I hunger for." He knew the great
novella *Tonio Kröger* (1903), but not *Buddenbrooks* (1901)
or *Death in Venice* (1911).

One imagines the *frisson fraternel* Kafka might have felt
upon encountering Conrad's *The Heart of Darkness* (1902)
and *The Secret Agent* (1907); André Gide's *L'immoraliste*
(1902); James Joyce's *Dubliners* (1914); and Rainer Maria
Rilke's *Auguste Rodin* (1903), *New Poems* (1907), and
The Notebooks of Malte Laurids Brigge (1910). *New Poems*
included "The Panther" and "The Swan," which might
have had special appeal for the author of "A Report to the
Academy," "Investigations of a Dog," and other stories
with animals as protagonists. He had not read any of them.
The only reference to Rilke in the correspondence occurs in
a letter to Felice, in which he mentions Rilke's having made
extremely kind remarks about "The Stoker," while neither
The Metamorphosis nor *In the Penal Colony* had "achieved
the same effect." (*LF*, 536) It seems that Kafka and Rilke
never met, although the poet was then living in Munich.
Rilke's interest in Kafka's work has been documented in
his correspondence with his publisher, Kurt Wolff, who
was also Kafka's first publisher.

Kafka was not musical. That would be a reason for his not
having heard—or, apparently, heard of—Richard Strauss's
Der Rosenkavalier (which had its premiere in Dresden in
1911) or *Ariadne auf Naxos* (first performed in 1912 in
Stuttgart), although he admired the librettist, Hugo von
Hofmannstahl. For that matter, there is no mention in his
diary or correspondence of Hofmannstahl's *Letter to Lord
Chandos* (published in 1902), which was widely debated as
an important modernist manifesto. But a comment, noted
by Janouch, suggests that Kafka had sympathy and a keen

eye for Picasso's work.[4] There is no indication that he was acquainted with the work of Cézanne or Matisse, or with the Cubist movement. As was also true, until his late period, of Henry James, another great modernist master—in James's case by reason of his temperament and artistic predilections, in Kafka's because of his life circumstances—Kafka had been cut off from many of the main artistic developments that shaped the cultural life of the twentieth century. The claustrophobia of the world portrayed in his fiction mirrors that of his own existence.

---

[4] Recalling a visit with Kafka to an exhibition of French painting, Janouch reports that, in answer to a comment he made on Picasso's "rose coloured women with gigantic feet," which was to the effect that Picasso was a "wilful distortionist," Kafka replied: "I do not think so.... He only registers the deformities which have not yet penetrated our consciousness. Art is a mirror, which goes 'fast,' like a watch—sometimes.'" (*J*, 143)

II

What have I in common with Jews?

Kafka's small urban universe remained stable. The German elementary school and German secondary school he attended were minutes away from his house, as was his university, Ferdinand-Karls Universität, also known as the Karolinum. His only two places of employment were likewise in the center of Prague: Assicurazioni Generali, at the corner of Heinrichgasse and Wenzelsplatz, and the Insurance Institute, on Poric. Only the tiny house in Alchimistengasse that Ottla rented as a place to escape her family (and perhaps to meet in secret with her future husband, Josef David) and allowed her brother to use for his writing in 1916 and 1917, and the apartment in the Schönborn Palace that Kafka took when he still thought that he would marry Felice, were across the Moldau, on Prague's aristocratic Kleinseite. The lodgings he occupied for short periods after 1914–10 Bilekgasse; his sister Valli's apartment; and the apartment he took on Langegasse in order not to interfere any longer with Valli and her family—were once again on the right bank of the Moldau, although farther from the center and, therefore, from the family apartment and the Institute than he had been used to.

To the centripetal forces—the work at the Institute to earn his living, and, riddled with contradictions, dependence on the family as well as aversion to risk—that held Kafka prisoner in Prague, must be added one more, which confined him in a world within a world, separate from others: anti-Semitism so pervasive in Bohemia that in their daily life Jews, even assimilated Jews like Kafka, took it for granted. How else could they have gone on? It was part of their landscape, no different in its permanence from the Charles Bridge, the Altstadt, the Hradceny Castle, and the Moldau. Kafka notes in his diary that "there were perhaps only two Jews in my class possessed of courage, and both shot themselves while still at school or shortly after."(*D*, 400) Jews who lacked that form of bravery swallowed hard and lived in a ghetto. Of course, it was no more impossible to leave that ghetto than it had been to leave Wossek, as proved by the emigration of members of the Kafka and Löwy families to the United States and other places far and wide, where anti-Semitism was thought to be less virulent.

But it wasn't easy to emigrate. A diary entry from 1912 shows how the Zionist solution, for instance, could seem unappealing to a sophisticated and skeptical Jew:

> This evening Dr. L. at our house. Another emigrant to Palestine. Is taking his bar examination a year before the end of his clerkship and is leaving (in two weeks) for Palestine with 1,200 K. Will try to get a position with the Palestine Office. All these emigrants to Palestine (Bergmann, Dr. Keller) have downcast eyes, feel blinded by their listeners, fumble around on the table with the tips of their extended fingers, their voices quiver, they smile weakly and prop up these smiles with a little irony. Dr. Keller told us that his students are chauvinists, have the Maccabees forever in their mouths and want to take after them. (*D*, 210)

In fact, few Jews in reasonably comfortable economic circumstances were ready to leave their Eastern European or Central European *Heimat* and trade security for the unknown. To provoke mass flight, persecution had to reach the pitch of the Nazi measures taken in Germany beginning in 1933. Even when confronted by them, however, many German Jews didn't leave, either because doors of countries to which they might flee (France, England, the United States) were closing, or because they couldn't believe what was happening to Jews all around them might also happen to them.

There would have been nothing surprising, therefore, to a Prague contemporary in the fact that Kafka's friends, a group of particularly talented and accomplished men— Oskar Pollak, Max Brod, Felix Weltsch, Oskar Baum, Franz Werfel, and Hugo Bergmann, among others—were exclusively Jewish. No Christian was ever included, whether German- or Czech-speaking. Brod's liaison with Emmy Salveter, a German actress whom Brod met when she was still a hotel chambermaid, and Kafka's passionate attachment to Milena Jesenská, a Czech-speaking Catholic, were both out of the ordinary. Kafka never let Milena forget the divide separating Jews from Christians, and one may suppose that in her letters to him, which have not been preserved, she gave him like for like. The only Christians with whom Kafka came into regular contact were colleagues at the Institute, his father's Czech employees, and, after his sister Ottla's marriage, her husband, Josef David. Kafka had stood by Ottla when she decided to marry him, in the face of their parents' bitter opposition. The marriage took place on July 15, 1920. More than a year before that, Kafka had written to her apropos of a remark by Brod to the effect that the marriage was a present and future loss for Jews:

> You know that you are doing something extraordi-
> nary, and that it is good to do the extraordinary, but
> also extraordinarily difficult. But if you never forget
> the responsibility for such a difficult action, if you
> remain aware that you are stepping out of line as

confidently, as say, David out of the army, and if in
spite of this awareness you keep believing that you
have the strength to carry the thing to a good end,
than you will have done more than if—to end with a
poor joke, if you had married ten Jews. (*LO*, 37)

Kafka got along well with David, and asked him to polish
letters he wrote in Czech to the Czech-speaking director
of the Insurance Institute, or simply asked him to translate
the German draft, but there is no indication that it occurred
to him that he might befriend other Christians, Czech
or German. It would have been an initiative that no one
expected, and one that apparently did not tempt him. His
astonishment at being in love with a Christian and being
loved by her is a leitmotif in his letters to Milena.

Although it doesn't appear that Kafka was ever the target
of an anti-Semitic insult or assault, the air he breathed
was pregnant with them. Three "ritual murder trials,"
throwbacks to the Middle Ages, and unimaginable for Jews
believing that they lived in an era of moral as well as material
progress, took place within his lifetime. The first, the
Tiszaeszláer affair, was so named for the small Hungarian
town where on April 1, 1882, Eszter Solymosi, a fourteen-
year-old Christian servant girl, disappeared after being
sent on an errand. Stimulated by anti-Semitic politicians,
a rumor spread that she had been the victim of Jewish ritual
murder, a crime committed, according to superstition, in
order to obtain Christian blood for use in the preparation
of unleavened bread. That year, Passover happened to fall
on April 4, a circumstance that could be used to explain the
immediate need for the blood. Two Jewish boys, five and
thirteen years old, gave coerced testimony on the basis of
which a number of Jews, including three ritual butchers and
the boys' parents, were accused of the murder of Eszter at
the synagogue where the boys' father was a custodian. After

an investigation and legal proceedings that dragged on for over a year, in August 1883, all the accused were acquitted by a unanimous judgment of the court in Budapest (a month after Kafka was born). Their liberation was followed by widespread anti-Jewish rioting in Hungary. In 1916, Kafka read Arnold Zweig's play *Ritualmord in Ungarn* [Ritual Murder in Hungary], based on the Tiszaeszláer affair. Writing to Felice, he criticized the play with his usual asperity, but in conclusion told her:

> I no longer see him [Zweig] the way I used to. At one point I had to stop reading, sit down on the sofa, and weep. It's years since I wept. (*LF*, 530)

The accusations and the graphic details set out in the boys' testimony—they claimed that two of the butchers held down the girl while the third slit her throat—could not have failed to have a special meaning for the grandson of the butcher of Wossek. The act of butchering reverberates in his diary and in his work. In the diary entry for November 2, 1911, he wrote: "This morning, for the first time in a long time, the joy again of imagining a knife twisted in my heart." (*D*, 101) Even stranger, the entry for May 3, 1913, records:

> Always the image of a pork butcher's broad knife that quickly and with mechanical regularity chops into me from the side and cuts off very thin slices which fly off almost like shavings because of the speed of the action. (*D*, 221)

The nightmare or daydream recurs in the entry for September 16, 1915:

> Between throat and chin would seem to be the most rewarding place to stab. Lift the chin and stick the

knife into the tensed muscles. But this spot is probably rewarding only in one's imagination. You expect to see a magnificent rush of blood and a network of sinews and little bones like you find in the leg of a roast turkey. (*D*, 342)

And, of course, a "long, thin, double-edged butcher's knife" plunges into Joseph K.'s heart in *The Trial*. (*T*, 229) An even more brutal version occurs in his short story "Fratricide," published in Kafka's lifetime in the volume entitled *A Country Doctor*. The murderer, Schmar, calls to his victim:

"Wese!" shrieked Schmar, standing on tiptoe, his arm outstretched, the knife sharply lowered, "Wese! You will never see Julia again!" And right into the throat and left into the throat and a third time deep into the belly stabbed Schar's knife. Water rats, slit open, give out such a sound as came from Wese. (*CS*, 401)

Closer to home than Tiszaeszláer, 1897 ended in Bohemia with the so-called December storm: anti-German riots that quickly turned into a pogrom in Prague. During three days, mobs first vandalized noticeably German institutions and then pillaged Jewish shops, broke into synagogues, smashed thousands of windows, and assaulted anyone they identified as a Jew. Countless Jewish businesses were ruined. Herman Kafka's shop was spared, because the name, although probably derived from a diminutive of Yakov, the Hebrew form of Jacob, means in Czech jackdaw and, therefore, could be taken as having a Czech origin. Besides, Herman didn't look Jewish. Order was restored, but only after the government had declared martial law in the city and brought in troops. Kafka was already a secondary school student at the time. He could not have been unaware of these events or their impact.

Two years later, Bohemia had its own ritual murder case. On April 1, 1899, the day before Easter, nineteen-year-old Agnes Hruza was found dead on a country road near Polná, a small town in Bohemia. Her throat had been cut. There was no known motive and no likely suspect until the editor of a small anti-Semitic Czech paper in Prague pointed the finger at Leopold Hilsner, a local shoemaker's assistant. Anti-Jewish politicians and the yellow press in Bohemia and Vienna turned the judicial proceedings into a lynching. Once again allegations flew that cutting Agnes's throat was part of the preparation of unleavened bread for Passover. Unlike the accused in Tiszaeszláer, Hilsner was found guilty and sentenced to death. However, Thomas G. Masaryk, a philosophy professor and politician who would become the first president of independent Czechoslovakia, led a public campaign to reexamine the case. On retrial, Hilsner was once again found guilty and sentenced to be hanged, but in 1901 the sentence was commuted to life imprisonment and, in 1918 he was finally pardoned.

The Tiszaeszláer and Hilsner cases soon had their analogue in Russia. In 1911, a Jew by the name of Menahem Mendel Beilis, a father of five employed as the superintendent at a Kiev brick factory, was accused of the murder of a Christian child whose mutilated body was found in a cave near the factory. A Catholic priest brought in as an expert on Judaic rituals testified that all the characteristics of ritual murder were present. Beilis was held in jail for two years and then acquitted by a unanimous jury. The news, first of the accusation leveled against Beilis, and then of his release, set off a wave of ferocious pogroms throughout Ukraine. According to Dora Diamant, Kafka wrote a story about the Beilis case, the manuscript of which she burned in accordance with his instructions.

The ritual murder hysteria subsided in Bohemia, but economic pressures against Jews continued until the beginning of the World War and, if anything, became more pervasive. Organized boycotts of Jewish shops and Jewish lawyers and doctors were widespread, and gave a preview of the boycott of April 1, 1933, all across Germany, which was the first general anti-Jewish measure taken after the grant of dictatorial powers to Hitler by the German Reichstag.

More pernicious than the barriers that excluded Bohemian Jews from all but the lowest civil service positions and from university teaching positions were obstacles preventing their employment by German and Czech banks. In addition, there was a clamor for quota restrictions on admission of Jews to institutions of higher learning. With the beginning of World War I came a pause in the anti-Jewish agitation. Jews showed their patriotism by voluntarily enlisting and displaying courage on the battlefield: above all, Austrian and Bohemian Jewish communities feared a Russian victory and Russian-style pogroms if Russian troops entered Austro-Hungarian territory. Since Czech nationalists had pan-Slavic aspirations and sympathized with Russia, Austrian and Bohemian Jews' manifestly pro-Austrian position became another stimulant for Czech anti-Semitism. Emperor Franz Joseph died in 1916. Crown Prince Franz Ferdinand, who succeeded him, was well known to be anti-Semitic. For the older generation of Jews, the old emperor had remained the author and symbol of their emancipation. They felt bereft. With Franz Joseph gone, who was to watch over them?

It was a good question. The birth in November 1918 of the independent Republic of Czechoslovakia marked the beginning of a new phase of anti-Jewish turmoil. In May 1919 Jews were beaten in the streets of central Prague. The turmoil and vehement anti-Jewish propaganda continued through the year, with Jews roughed up and insulted in streets, parks, trolley cars, and public places. A climax was reached in Prague a year and a half later. On November 16, 1920, during a day of particularly severe rioting, the mob stormed the Jewish Rathaus, the center of the Jewish community, devastated Jewish archives, and trampled on Torahs. Kafka reported to Milena on a riot he had seen:

> I've been spending every afternoon outside in the streets, wallowing in anti-Semitic hate. The other day I heard someone call the Jews a "mangy race." Isn't it natural to leave a place where one is so hated? (Zionism or national feeling isn't needed for this at all.) The heroism of staying is nonetheless merely the heroism of cockroaches which cannot be exterminated, even from the bathroom.
>
> I've just looked out the window: mounted police, gendarmes with fixed bayonets, a screaming mob dispersing, and up here in the window the unsavory shame of living under constant protection. (*LM*, 212–3)

There is a price exacted from those who live in a place where they are rejected and openly hated by their neighbors: loss of confidence in one's identity and its corollary, the unending need for self-reinvention. Kafka wrote to Milena twice during that November about the "one peculiarity" which distinguished him from all the people he knew, not in essence, but very much in degree:

> After all, we both know numerous typical examples of the Western Jew; as far as I know, I'm the most Western-Jewish of them all. In other words, to exaggerate, not one second of calm has been granted me; nothing has been granted me, everything must be earned, not only the present and future, but the past as well—something that is, perhaps, given every human being—this too must be earned, and this probably entails the hardest work of all. If the Earth turns to

the right—I'm not sure it does—then I would have to turn to the left to make up for the past. But as it is I don't have the least bit of strength for these obligations; I can't carry the world on my shoulders—I can barely carry my winter coat....On my own, I can't go the way I want—I can't even want to do so. I can only be quiet; I can't want anything else, and I don't want anything else. (*LM*, 217–8)

Then, abruptly, he proposed an image of himself

as a person...constantly missing everything he needs to take with him, and so each time he has to sew his clothes, make his boots, manufacture his walking stick, etc. Of course, it's impossible to do all of that well; it may hold up for a few blocks, but then suddenly, on the Graben, for example, everything falls apart and he's left standing there naked with rags and pieces. And now the torture of running back to the Altstädter Ring [the address of Kafka's parents' apartment]! And in the end he runs into an angry mob on the Eisengasse, hot in pursuit of Jews.

Don't misunderstand me, Milena, I'm not saying such a man is lost, not at all, but he is lost the minute he goes to the Graben where he is a disgrace to himself and the world. (*LM*, 217)

The opposite of the "most Western Jewish man of them all" persona, which Kafka did not particularly like, was that of the Eastern European Jew. Writing to Felice about her volunteer work with Eastern European Jewish children at the Jewish People's Home in Berlin, which she had undertaken at his urging, he had told her that "I can think of no closer spiritual bond between us than that created by that work," and stated the goal of the Home, as he understood it: to imbue the children with the mode of life of the volunteers. "Since people are sewn into their skins for life and cannot alter any of the seams," he continued,

> one will try to raise them to the standard of the contemporary, educated, West European Jew, Berlin version, which admittedly may be the best of its kind. With that, not much would be achieved. If, for instance, I had to choose between the Berlin Home and another where the pupils were the Berlin helpers (dearest, even with you among them, and with me, no doubt, at the head), and the helpers simple East European Jews from Kolomyja or Stanslawow, I would give unconditional preference to the latter Home.... But I don't think this choice exists; no one has it; the quality corresponding to the value of the East European Jew is something that cannot be imparted in a Home. (*LF*, 500)

He recognized "that the work in the Home derives from Zionism...it kindles national aspirations by invoking the ancient prodigious past" but cautioned Felice that "I am not a Zionist." (*LF*, 501) Presumably that left him with the sour self-assessment made in 1914 in the course of explaining to Grete Bloch why his marrying Felice was "no mean venture." He was, he then told her, a completely antisocial man in an indifferent state of health hard to determine at the moment, excluded from every great soul-sustaining community on account of his "non-Zionist (I admire Zionism and am nauseated by it), non-practicing Judaism..." (*LF*, 423) His views were nothing if not consistent. A year earlier, he told Max Brod that the Zionist Congress he attended in September 1913 in Vienna "was all useless business... I sat in on the Zionist Congress as if it were an event totally alien to me." (*L*, 100) But he didn't give up on Eastern Jewish spirituality: a few days later, he told Felice to get her pupils to trust her in other than religious matters and "let the dark complexity of Judaism, which contains so many impenetrable features, do its work." (*LF*, 502)

Whatever might be said of the metaphoric man on the Graben whom Kafka had evoked for Milena, his own case was far graver. Writing was his religion; his clothes, boots, and walking stick were the German language in which he wrote and the German culture that continued to nourish him. His education had been purely German; he looked on Goethe as his literary ancestor, and Kleist, Hebbel, and Grillparzer as fraternal spirits. Learning to speak German had been his father's ticket from Wossek to Prague. It made it possible for him to leave the life of a peddler for what seemed to be a higher form of existence: that of a secular, respected, and reasonably prosperous merchant in Prague, well able to send to the university *Herr Sohn*—as he called Kafka when he wished to taunt him. His commitment to the life he had made for himself was unequivocal, as unequivocal as his matter-of-fact commitment to his Jewish identity. But Kafka had not been obliged to claw his way out of a rural ghetto. He had become assimilated as the natural consequence of the time, place, and social class into which he had been born. As late as in January 1914, he was able to ask the following rhetorical question:

What have I in common with Jews? I have hardly anything in common with myself, and should stand very quietly in a corner, content that I can breathe. (*D*, 252)

The Czech-speaking factotum's presence in the Kafka household and the Czech lessons notwithstanding, German was the Kafka children's primary language. Since ninety-three percent of Prague's population was Czech-speaking, as was the majority of the clientele of the family shop—in which his parents and Ottla worked, and where Kafka at times had to give a hand—Czech was the language of the family business. German was its language of intimacy. All the same, in the fall of 1911, a year during which Kafka was tormented by paroxysms of doubt about his relation to the language of which, as would soon be revealed, he was a great master, he wrote in his diary:

> Yesterday it occurred to me that I did not always love my mother as she deserved and as I could, only because the German language prevented it. The Jewish mother is no "Mutter," to call her "Mutter" makes her a little comical (although not to her, since we are in Germany[sic in the original]). We give a Jewish woman the name of a German mother, but forget the contradiction that sinks into the emotions so much more heavily, "Mutter" is peculiarly German for the Jew, it unconsciously contains, together with the Christian splendor, Christian coldness also, the Jewish woman who is called "Mutter" therefore becomes not only comical but strange. Mama would be a better name only if one didn't imagine "Mutter" behind it. I believe that it is only the memories of the ghetto that still preserve the Jewish family, for the word "Vater" too is far from meaning the Jewish father. (*D*, 88)

A reasonable solution for the problem, one might think, would have been to use for the father a Yiddish diminutive, *tateleben*, which Kafka surely knew. His parents, especially his father, did not hesitate to use Yiddish expressions in private. 1911 was also a year when Kafka became steeped in the lore of the Lemberg Yiddish theater, which was performing in Prague. He sought the company of the Yiddish actors, especially Yitzhak Löwy, and developed a crush on one of the actresses, the overblown Frau Tschissik. Isaac Bashevis Singer later mocked this infatuation in his story "A Friend of Kafka." He had also begun to read Heinrich Graetz's *History of Jews*. It was at first stranger to him than he had expected, and he "had to stop here and there in order by resting to allow my Jewishness to collect itself."(*D*, 99). Within a few months, on February 18, 1912, he delivered a remarkable speech introducing a Yiddish poetry reading by Löwy at Prague's Toynbee Hall on February 18, 1912. He told his audience that anyone who spoke German was also capable of understanding Yiddish:

> once Yiddish has taken hold of you and moved you—and Yiddish is everything, the words, the Chasidic melody, and the essential character of this East European Jewish actor himself—you will have forgotten your former reserve. Then you will come to feel the true unity of Yiddish, and so strongly that it will frighten you, yet it will no longer be fear of Yiddish but of yourselves. (*RK*, 286)

The rub was there. Kafka knew that the assimilated Jews sitting in Toynbee Hall feared close contact with their grandparents' language, and most likely deep down he feared it as well. Of course neither Kafka nor the other Jews he was addressing were afraid of being identified as Jews: they weren't trying to pass as Christians, if only because it would have been impossible to do so in Prague, where everyone in the German-speaking minority knew everyone else. Rather, the fear was of a crack in the veneer of assimilation through which might enter the miasma of the shtetl or the medieval ghetto that had been left behind, the heritage that these Jews had recently and completely cast aside. For Kafka, Yiddish and the shtetl held out the attraction of the close-knit spiritual community that he imagined flourished there and, I believe, a special terror: that of further linguistic alienation.

Times had changed. Initially, assimilation had seemed to follow naturally from the emancipation of Jews: it had been perceived as the essential element enabling them to take their rightful place as full members of the secular society. However, in the last decades of the nineteenth century, it had come under attack by nationalists and racists as a Jewish trick involving the theft of German national identity and the pollution of German culture by alien and despised outsiders. Most importantly for Kafka, it was argued that the "theft" could not result in genuine possession of the purloined language. No Jew could write great works of prose or poetry in German, any more than he could compose great music. Likewise, Jews were not capable of becoming great performers of music, especially singers. The doors of high artistic achievement were closed to them because as a race, and by reason of their despised traditional employments, they were not creative. The accusation was unbearable and also manifestly foolish, but Kafka, like many other Jews, at times felt guilty as charged.

To this had to be added the special problems caused by the German spoken in Prague by the small and isolated, although still ascendant, German minority. The linguistic situation was described by Fritz Mauthner (1849–1923), a German writer and student of language, born in Bohemia:

> The Germans in the inner parts of Bohemia, sur-
> rounded by Czechs, speak a paper German [*papiernes
> Deutsch*] that lacks the fullness of organic expression
> and spoken forms. The melody of the spoken language
> has also been lost. (*RK*, 39)

An anecdote Kafka recounted to Brod illustrates the odd linguistic position of Prague's German speakers. In the spring of 1920, while in Merano, a mountain station in the Alto Adige region of Italy, on medical leave necessitated by his tuberculosis, Kafka stayed at the Pension Ottoburg. The guests there were all German and Christian—a new experience for him. He had asked to be served at a separate little table in the dining room, so that his vegetarian diet would attract less attention, and he could "Fletcherize" to his heart's content without making a spectacle of himself and disgusting his fellow diners. But he was talked into joining the common table, and thus became the subject of an interrogation by the Austrian general and colonel who were also staying at the Pension and knew something about Prague. Kafka explained that he wasn't Czech. However, he wrote to Brod,

> the general, with his sharp ears linguistically schooled in the Austrian army, was not satisfied. After we had eaten, he once more began to wonder about the sound of my German, perhaps more bothered by what he saw than by what he heard. At this point I tried to answer him, explaining I was Jewish. At this his scientific curiosity, to be sure, was satisfied, but not his human feelings. At this same moment, probably by sheer chance, for all the others could not have heard our conversation, but perhaps there was some connection after all, the whole company rose to leave....The general, too, was very restless, though from politeness he brought our little chat to a sort of end before he hurried out with long strides. That hardly satisfied my human feelings either; why must I be a thorn in their flesh? (*L*, 233)

Kafka's accent wasn't Jewish; he spoke with the hard accent referred to by Mauthner that was common to Prague and other Bohemian speakers of German, Jews and gentiles alike. The high German purism of Kafka's prose, the austerity of his language, and the occasional peculiarities of his spelling and usage were also products of his Prague upbringing.

But the general had touched a nerve. "Why should the Jews be so irresistibly drawn to [the German] language?" Kafka wrote to Brod one year later, from a sanatorium in Matliary. The impetus was a discussion of *mauscheln* in a book by Karl Kraus, a converted Jew of Bohemian origin and brilliant satirist. *Mauscheln* was a subspecies of German spoken by Jews, comparable to the English once heard on Upper Broadway. Kafka moved quickly to a larger issue: the relationship of assimilated Jews to the German literature. The contribution Jews had made was in his opinion insignificant, if not negative. The reason could be found in the "frightful inner predicament" of assimilated young Jews wishing to write and to leave their fathers' Jewishness—a wish in which the fathers connived—but unable to do so for "with their posterior legs they were still glued to their father's Jewishness, and with their waving anterior legs they found no new ground." The result was an impasse:

> The impossibility of not writing, the impossibility of writing German, the impossibility of writing differently. One might also add a fourth impossibility, the impossibility of writing....Thus what has resulted was a literature impossible in all respects, a gypsy literature which had stolen the German child out of its cradle and in great haste put it through some kind of training, for someone had to dance on the tightrope. (But it wasn't a German child, it was nothing; people merely said that somebody was dancing). (*L*, 288–9)

It was impossible for Kafka not to write. But it was a consequence of not acting on the question that he had put to Milena, "isn't it natural to leave a place where one is so hated," that this great master of German prose should have been brought to ponder "the impossibility of writing German" for the simple reason that he was a Jew, or to assert, even if only to score a point in his letter to a close friend, that his works were part of "a gypsy literature which had stolen the German child."

Unquestionably, the sense that his creative powers had waned or perhaps deserted him, and consciousness of the ravages of tuberculosis, both added to the weight of Kafka's despair. He knew that he wasn't getting well and probably never would. Since the winter of 1917–18, when he was thirty-four, he had written nothing more substantial than aphorisms and the *Letter to His Father*, a magnificent prose work but a private document that he wouldn't have considered part of his literary production. Giving it to Milena, he told her that he didn't want anyone other than her to read it. (*LM*, 63) He had abandoned his diary entirely in 1918—a matter of considerable significance to him since the diary so often was a bridge to his fiction—and hardly wrote in it in 1919 and 1920. All his energy had seemingly passed into compulsive letter writing. He started *The Castle* in 1922 and was unable to finish it, and in the remaining year and a half of his life he wrote two of his most beautiful stories, "The Hunger Artist" and "Josephine, the Singer, or the Mouse Folk," both of which he deemed fit for publication. That was, however, a burst of activity that he had not expected: in the meantime, he had come to fear that he lacked authenticity. No greater torment for a writer can be imagined.

Kafka was a master dialectician and seldom found himself on only one side of an argument. His insistence that he was not a Zionist was counterbalanced by his often misty-eyed admiration of the spiritual qualities of Eastern Jews, and his urging others, notably Felice Bauer and his friend Robert Klopstock, to become involved in Zionist causes. Such contradictions, his intermittent self-lacerating and provocative pronouncements about his relation to Jews as a group; his qualms, real or feigned, about the legitimacy of the use by Jewish writers of the German language; as well as what some have diagnosed as his attempts to differentiate himself from the stereotypical Jew of anti-Semitic propaganda, have been used by scholars to buttress the argument that Kafka was himself a Jewish anti-Semite, a self-hating Jew.

The accusation is unfair and, in the end, beside the point. Certainly, Kafka saw the chasm separating him from Eastern Jews. It was the inescapable result of the social progress of his family from ritual butchering in Wossek to a bourgeois existence in Prague financed by a more refined trade, and the concomitant process of assimilation. Kafka's education had been secular and Western; he was a man of great culture and considerable personal refinement and reserve. It would have been surprising if he, who was so repelled by his own father's vulgarity at table and in speech, had not been similarly repelled by the oddities of dress, habits, gestures, and speech of the very Jews of whom he made a fetish, because of the community spirit, cohesiveness, and genuine emotional warmth he was convinced they possessed.

Nothing shows more clearly the duality of Kafka's view of Eastern European Jewish life than his description of the circumcision ceremony in Russia, apparently related to him by the actor Yitzhak Löwy, the joyousness and spontaneity of which had fascinated him. He compared it favorably with the artificiality of the same ceremony performed a day earlier on his nephew Felix, at which "those present, aside from the grandfathers, spent the time in dreams or boredom with a complete lack of understanding the prayer." That did not prevent him from noting the revolting aspect of the Russian bris, as when he observes that Russian circumcisers

all have red noses and reeking breath. It is therefore not very pleasant when, after the operation has been performed, they suck the bloody member with this mouth, in the prescribed manner. The member is then sprinkled with sawdust and heals in about three days. (*D*, 152)

He followed that description with one concerning the study of the Talmud, an activity that he thought was at the core of Russian Jews' spiritual life:

they come together at every possible opportunity, whether to pray or to study or to discuss divine matters or to eat holiday meals whose basis is usually a religious one and at which alcohol is drunk only very moderately. *They flee to one another, so to speak* [emphasis added]. (*D*, 152)

This was a concept that a man as private and withdrawn as Kafka could admire, but only from a distance. He does not differ much in this respect from countless successful and cultivated children or grandchildren of emigrants from the "old country," drawn by nostalgia to visit their family village before progress and globalization had homogenized it. The admiration for tradition-laden customs and unsophisticated directness has not always been sufficient to obscure the other side of the coin: primitive and unsanitary living conditions, and the cloying familiarity of newly discovered aunts, uncles, and distant cousins.

Walter Benjamin (1892–1940), the celebrated essayist, critic, and translator, was a German Jew from Berlin born into a wealthy and assimilated family. An early admirer of Kafka, he wrote about him with great sensitivity and insight. Hannah Arendt (1907–75), also Jewish, was born in Germany and trained there as a philosopher. Both Benjamin and Arendt left Germany for France to escape Nazi persecution. Arendt was able to emigrate to the United States in 1941 and settled in New York City. Benjamin committed suicide on September 27, 1940, in a hotel room in Portbou, in the Pyrenees, having found that Spanish border police would not honor the visa he held and allow him to enter Spain. In an introduction to a selection of Benjamin's essays, Arendt discussed the "Jewish question" as it presented itself to assimilated German Jews of his generation. Kafka and Benjamin were near enough contemporaries for Arendt's comments to be considered directly relevant to Kafka's situation, and entitled to great weight:

> ...the insolubility of the Jewish question for that generation consisted not only in their speaking and writing German or in the fact that their "production plant" was located in Europe—in Benjamin's case in Berlin West [a residential part of Berlin] or in Paris, something about which he did "not have the slightest illusions."...What was decisive was that these men did not wish to "return" either to the ranks of the Jewish people or to Judaism, and could not desire to do so—not because they believed in "progress" and an automatic disappearance of anti-Semitism or because they were too "assimilated" and too alienated from their Jewish heritage, but because all traditions and cultures as well as all "belonging" had become equally questionable to them. This is what they felt was wrong with the "return" to the Jewish fold as proposed by the Zionists; they could all have said what Kafka once said about being a member of the Jewish people: "My people, provided that I have one."[5]

---

5   Hannah Arendt, in the introduction to Walter Benjamin's *Illuminations: Essays and Reflections* (New York: Schocken Books, 1968), p. 36.

The Jewish stereotype disseminated by anti-Semitic propaganda strung together a variety of insults. They ranged from the abstract through the crudely physical. Jews were money changers and usurers, peddlers, innkeepers, cobblers, and so forth, averse to any form of manual labor, unproductive and uncreative, overly intellectual, unsuited for military service; smaller and weaker than Aryans (but oddly prone to sexual voracity), big-nosed, hollow-chested, flat-footed, tubercular, prone to insanity, and so on. Stereotypes often contain a grain of disagreeable truth. Having been for centuries excluded from ownership of land and confined in ghettoes, Jews indeed were no longer tillers of the land or herders of flocks. The callings they could pursue were perforce those of the stereotype. The way of life connected with those callings, and the ghetto and shtetl conditions in which they were conducted, did not lead to development of physical strength and vigor, so that nineteenth-century racists were able to back up theories of Jewish racial inferiority with a plethora of studies measuring such characteristics as height, weight, chest expansion, muscle strength, and the incidence of tuberculosis, syphilis, heart disease, and mental illness.

These traits, which made the stereotype loathsome, were the very ones that early Zionism tried to alter radically with its emphasis on physical training and the creation in Palestine of a society based on kibbutz ideals of farming the land, craftsmanship, and self-defense. It is nonsense to suggest for that reason that Zionism was an anti-Semitic movement of self-hating Jews. However, Zionists did want to leave the ghetto behind, and their goal was to transform a Jewish people, burdened by the history of odious discrimination and violence against them inflicted by communities in the midst of which they lived, into a proudly independent nation. Kafka's efforts to learn to swim and row, to perform Müller exercises (a popular Danish system of gymnastics he had been practicing since 1909) year-round in the nude—before an open window—to garden and learn carpentry, were not unreasonable means of improving his physical condition, which he considered "a major obstacle to my progress" (*D*, 124), and momentarily escaping the suffocating atmosphere of the family apartment, the Institute, and Prague's café life.

The cumulative effect on Kafka of the ubiquitous anti-Semitism—not only in Prague but seemingly wherever he turned—was necessarily profound. It resulted in what can only be described as profound fatigue. Other people— so it sometimes seems to a Jew—do not need to spend their lives justifying their right to exist, or, if that right is conceded, questioning the legitimacy of their writing, musical composition, or singing onstage. It is that fatigue that underlies Kafka's outburst in a letter to Milena:

> at times I'd like to stuff them all, simply as Jews (me included) into, say, the drawer of the laundry chest. Next I'd wait, open the drawer a little to see if they've suffocated, and if not, shut the drawer again and keep doing this to the end. (*LM*, 46)

And doubtless it contributed to his bleak vision of the incomprehensible, cruel, and unjust forces to which humanity is subject. How could it have failed to do so? But to read Kafka's fiction as tales and parables of anti-Semitic experience garnished with knowing winks directed at a Jewish audience is to underestimate him. In his fiction he transcended his Jewish experience and his Jewish identity. He wrote about the human condition.

III

The deeper realm of real sexual life is closed to me...

A man of thirty who writes a letter to a young woman asking her to marry him, follows it up with letters explaining that he is unsuited for marriage, and eight weeks later expresses the following sentiments in his diary, has an attitude toward women that is at best uneasy:

> 13 August. Perhaps everything is now ended and the letter I wrote yesterday was the last one. That would certainly be the best. What I shall suffer, what she will suffer—that cannot be compared with the common suffering that would result. I shall gradually pull myself together, she will marry, that is the only way out among the living.... She will realize this from my last letters. If not, then I will certainly marry her, for I am too weak to resist her opinion about our common fortune and am unable not to carry out, as far as I can, something that she considers possible.
>
> 14 August. The opposite has happened. There were three letters. The last letter I could not resist. I love her as far as I am capable of it, but the love lies buried to the point of suffocation under fear and self-reproaches...
>
> Coitus as punishment for the happiness of being together. Live as ascetically as possible, more ascetically than a bachelor, that is the only possible way for me to endure marriage. But she? (*D*, 227–8)

Conflicted certainly, but not indifferent to women or their sexual appeal. Aside from moments of triumph in which he wrote his best works, and, beginning in 1917, the milestones marking the progress of his disease, the events in Kafka's life that stand out are the peripeties of his pursuit of women followed by frantic attempts to escape. Two of his loves, Felice Bauer and Milena Jesenská, have been immortalized in letters to them that he had wanted destroyed. There are others who are important: Dora Diamant, the Polish-Jewish girl who cast her lot with Kafka at the end of the summer of 1923; little Julie Wohryzek, his fiancée during a brief period that followed the final break with Felice and ended upon Milena's entry on stage in 1920; the young Christian girl on whom he had a crush during a two-week stay in a sanatorium in Riva in the autumn of 1913; Hedwig Weiler, a young student from Vienna, whom he met in Triesch during the summer of 1907; and a mysterious, never identified mature woman who was his fellow patient in 1905 at a sanatorium in Zuckmantel.

There was also a shopgirl. Paradoxically, the only account of her is to be found in the letter Kafka wrote to Milena on August 8–9, 1920, in an attempt to explain the dichotomy in his psychological makeup between *strach* ("fear" in Czech) and *toucha* ("longing"). Milena's letters to Kafka having been lost, we don't know the question he was answering. It seems likely, however, that it had a close connection with Kafka's having delayed a disastrous meeting in Gmünd, a border town roughly halfway between Vienna and Prague, that ultimately took place on August 14–15. He told her that he had " 'feared' a night in Gmünd, but this was only the usual 'fear' (which unfortunately is quite sufficient) I have in Prague as well; it wasn't any special fear of Gmünd." He had already explained that "if we restrict 'fear' and 'longing' the way you do in your last letter, the question is not easy, but very simple to answer. *In that case I ONLY have fear."* (*LM*, 146)

The genesis of the dichotomy, he went on to tell her, was an incident involving a shopgirl who worked in a clothing store across from his family apartment when he was preparing for his first state examination in law. Using sign language that must have been very expressive they came to an understanding: he would pick her up at closing time. He was there outside the shop as agreed, but so was another man, whose arm she took. There were more signs from the girl that he correctly interpreted as asking him to follow them. After a halt at a beer garden, where Kafka sat at an adjoining table, the couple continued their walk until they arrived, Kafka still in tow, at the building where the girl lived. The other man said goodbye, the girl ran into the house, and Kafka waited. Soon she reappeared and without further ado they went to a hotel on the Kleinseite. "It was all enticing, exciting, and disgusting, even before we reached the hotel, and it wasn't any different inside," he told Milena. Later, he realized that "I was actually happy, but this happiness was only because my eternally grieving body had given me some peace at last, and above all because the whole thing had not been *more* disgusting, *more* dirty than it was." They saw each other once more, two days later, then he left for the country, and after that he could never bear the sight of the shopgirl, who was clearly puzzled by the change in his attitude. The reason known to him, though it was not the sole reason, was that she had done something slightly disgusting in the hotel (not worth mentioning), had said something slightly obscene. That something was enough to tell him that

deep down, this disgust and filth were a necessary part of the whole, and it was precisely this (which she had indicated to me by one slight action, one small word) which had drawn me with such amazing force into this hotel, which I would have otherwise avoided with all my remaining strength.

And it's stayed that way ever since. My body, often quiet for years, would then again be shaken by this longing for some very particular, trivial disgusting thing, something slightly repulsive, embarrassing, obscene, which I always found even in the best of cases—some insignificant odor, a little bit of sulphur, a little bit of hell. (*LM*, 146–7)

The meaning of that marvelous piece of prose may come down to something simple: the aspects of the sexual act that repelled and "frightened" Kafka were the same ones that were necessary for the awakening and perhaps also maintenance of his desire.

In the case of strictly transient relations with women— the shopgirl, waitresses, etc.—there wouldn't be enough time for the disgust mixed with *strach* to overcome the *toucha* associated with it. In longer-term relationships, the situation quickly became precarious. For instance, the liaisons in Zuckmantel (with a mature woman) and Riva (with the young Christian girl), occurring as they did outside Kafka's everyday Prague life, and not exceeding a few weeks in potential duration, did not plunge him into a panic. On the contrary, looked at from his point of view, they had been perfect, and remained his gold standard, against which would be tested even the one remarkable success in his relationship with Felice, which he attained during a brief stay with her in Marienbad in July 1916.

Unlike those two romanticized perfect adventures, the relationship with Hedwig Weiler, the girl he met in Triesch, exceeded the time limit. While the twenty-four-year-old Kafka was spending part of his 1907 summer vacation in

Triesch at his uncle's, Hedwig and he were the best of friends, and perhaps even lovers. Afterward, they went home, she to Vienna and Kafka to Prague, and letters took the place of physical flirtation. That was satisfactory from Kafka's point of view; he was in love and happy. The relationship began to cool when Hedwig came to Prague to continue her studies. That had not been included in the program: she was to have stayed in Vienna, while he nourished implausible hopes of going to Vienna himself to attend a business school specializing in export-import trade. With Hedwig actually installed in his own city, he had to face the need to carry their intimacy to some higher level, or at least maintain it. When he wrote to her in early 1908, a few months after her arrival in Prague, he was all reluctance and ice. One senses that his teeth were clenched. A year passed and the salutation was no longer "*Du, Liebe* [you, love]." He had retreated to the formal *Sie*, saluted her as "*Geehrtes* [honored] *Fräulein*," and announced that he was returning all her letters. He was proving the truth of an axiom he would propound in his diary years later: "I would never have married a girl with whom I had lived in the same city for a year." (*D*, 223)

The woman he spent almost five years trying to marry, much of that time using his lawyer's polemical skills to persuade her that their marriage would be disastrous, for months on end writing to her at least once a day, was Felice Bauer (1887–1960), born in Neustadt, in Upper Silesia (now Prudnik, in Poland). Two of her four siblings, Erna and Ferdinand ("Ferry"), are mentioned in the diaries and in the correspondence with some frequency: Erna, because she had befriended Kafka, particularly during the crisis of July 1914, when his first engagement to Felice was broken, leading him to believe that she understood him and might be on his side; and Ferry because his financial dealings were a source of problems for Felice and the rest of the family. The Bauers had moved from Neustadt to Berlin in 1899. Herr Bauer, an insurance agent, had caused problems as well: for six years, until 1910, he had kept a mistress and lived with her in another neighborhood in Berlin. Maintaining two households had been a heavy financial burden; as a result, the family's finances were shaky. In order to provide another income, in 1908 Felice left the business school she had been attending and went to work as a shorthand typist for a gramophone record firm. A year later she joined Carl Lindström A.G., a maker and distributor of dictaphones, and did so well that within a short time she was promoted. By the time Kafka met her, she had become a manager at the firm (*Prokuristin*). It was part of Kafka's misguided attachment to Felice that he admired—or professed to admire—her talent for business and efficiency, as well as other qualities that, however praiseworthy as a general matter, made her irremediably unsuitable as his marriage partner.

Their first meeting took place the evening of August 13, 1912, at the apartment of Max Brod's parents. Felice had stopped in Prague on her way to Budapest to attend a sister's wedding and called on the Brods. She had a family connection to them: her cousin, Max Friedmann, was married to Max Brod's sister Sophie. The married couple lived in Berlin and Felice was friendly with them. Kafka, a frequent visitor at the Brods', had come to the apartment to review with Max the order of eighteen of his short prose pieces that were to appear in the small volume eventually published by Rowohlt as *Meditation* [*Betrachtung*] 1913. He was having second thoughts about the wisdom of the project, and, in a moment of jitters experienced by most writers, he wrote in his diary: "If Rowohlt would send it back I could lock it up again as if it had all never happened so that I should be only as unhappy as I was before." (*D*,

207) Felice's presence frustrated the purpose of Kafka's visit. The conversation revolved instead around photographs taken during Kafka's and Brod's trip the previous month to Weimar, the plays Felice had seen, her job, the Brod and Bauer families, and Zionism. It transpired that Felice had studied Hebrew and was a Zionist, whereupon Kafka, in a moment of singular daring, proposed that next year they go to Palestine together. She agreed, and they shook hands to seal the bargain. Here is how he described the young woman one week later:

> Miss F.B. When I arrived at Brod's she was sitting at the table and I took her to be a servant. I was not at all curious about who she was, but rather took her for granted at once. Bony, empty face that wore its emptiness openly. Bare throat. A blouse thrown on. Looked very domestic in her dress although, as it later turned out, she by no means was. (I alienate myself from her a little by inspecting her so closely. What a state I'm in now, indeed, alienated from the whole of everything good, and don't believe it yet...) Almost broken nose. Blonde, somewhat straight, unattractive hair, strong chin. As I was taking my seat I looked at her closely for the first time, by the time I was seated I already had an unshakable opinion. (*D*, 207)

He enlarged on the description in an astonishing letter to her several weeks later—at the earliest stage of their correspondence—in which "to counter [her] remark that little notice had been taken of [her] that evening," he gave proof of total recall. He remembered it all, down to Frau Brod's slippers that Felice padded around in because her shoes had gotten wet in the rain, her crossed legs and way of plucking at her hair while someone played the piano, and the embarrassing moment when, upon arriving at the hotel where she was staying, the Brods and he having accompanied her, he crowded into her section of the revolving door and very nearly trod on her feet. (*LF*, 16–7) The first of his letters, formal and stilted, was written on September 20. He used as his opening gambit the promise she had made to accompany him to the Holy Land:

> Now, if you still wish to undertake this journey—you said at the time you are not fickle, and I saw no signs of it in you—then it will be not only right but absolutely essential to start discussing this journey at once. (*LF*, 5)

In reality, no such pretext was required to legitimize the correspondence. Felice was twenty-five and Kafka twenty-nine. According to the mores of the Jewish middle class, it was high time for them—especially Felice—to marry, and an epistolary courtship following an introduction, whether planned or fortuitous, at the home of family members or friends, was an accepted road to matrimony. Kafka's letter was unusual only in the level of anxiety detectable behind the screen of the visit to Palestine, and his disingenuous warning about his habits as a correspondent:

> I am an erratic letter writer....On the other hand, I never expect a letter to be answered by return; even when awaiting a letter day after day with renewed anticipation, I am never disappointed when it doesn't come, and when finally it does come, I am inclined to be startled. (*LF*, 5)

The opposite was true: Kafka wrote letters compulsively and copiously and turned into a hysterical despot if they were not answered forthwith, bombarding Felice with cables and remonstrances. Had he been as modern as Felice, he would have telephoned, with the result that his persistence would have been even more intolerable, although less well-documented.

Two days after the first letter to Felice was dispatched, working without interruption through the night Kafka wrote "The Judgment," an experience so powerful that he noted in his diary: "Only *in this way* can writing be done, only with such coherence, with such a complete opening out of the body and soul." (*D*, 213) He would dedicate the story, when it was published, to Felice. Her initials, F.B., are the same as those of the fiancée in "The Judgment," Frieda Brandenfeld. In hindsight, some ten months after the fact, Kafka considered that he was "indirectly in her debt for the story." (*D*, 228)

It does not take much delving into the correspondence for Kafka's more disturbing personality traits and patterns of behavior to come to the fore. Anxiety about the significance of a tardy reply—is she ill, had her or his letter been mis-addressed or lost, had he done something to offend her, was there some other reason for her failure to respect the imperatives of their epistolary relationship, such as the obligation to answer his letters by return mail—and nagging become a constant of their correspondence. We find Kafka taking the extraordinary step, almost unthinkable given his usual timidity, of asking Sophie Friedmann, Brod's sister, to intercede with her cousin by marriage, and convince her to answer one of his letters. When the wished-for reply finally arrives, and he has been told that an earlier letter has in fact been lost, he expresses satisfaction and, at the same time, calls her to order:

> This early stumble in our correspondence may have been quite a good thing; at least I know now that, even if letters get lost, I am allowed to write to you. But this must be the end to letters getting lost. (*LF*, 11)

But the hysterical outbursts and reproaches do not end:

> Dearest, what have I done that makes you torment
> me so? No letter again today, neither by the first mail
> nor the second. You do make me suffer.... If I am to
> go on living at all, I cannot go on vainly waiting for
> news of you, as I have done these last few interminable
> days. (*LF*, 50–1)

The pattern keeps on repeating itself with deadly monotony
until the correspondence finally ends in 1917, five years
after it began.

Another jarring note that will recur is sounded already
in the second letter: it is Kafka's obsessive intrusiveness. He
asks Felice to keep "a little diary" for him:

> You must record, for instance, at what time you get to
> the office, what you had for breakfast, what you see
> from your office window, what kind of work you do
> there, the names of your male and female friends, why
> you get presents, who tries to undermine your health by
> giving you sweets, and the thousand things of whose
> existence and possibilities I know nothing. (*LF*, 7)

This strange blend of voyeurism and the need to control
become increasingly egregious: he urges Felice to go to the
gym twice a week, to avoid needlework, and abstain from
taking Pyramidon for the headaches he fears are caused by
her staying up late to write to him. (*LF*, 19) He cautions
her against seeing too many people and handing out her
photograph to mere acquaintances (*LF*, 29), and wonders
whether it wouldn't be better for her to spend the summer
in a sanatorium than to carry on with her own vacation
plans. (*LF*, 63) He advises her not to jump off moving
trams and asks whether she has been to see the oculist;

(*LF*, 31) discourages her from drinking tea, recommending milk as a substitute, and worries about the quality of food available to her at the office. (*LF*, 163) In the midst of a serious crisis in their relations precipitated by his fear that she has cooled toward him, he reminds her that she had promised to begin to do Müller exercises and report on them continually. (*LF*, 299)

It takes Kafka five weeks to progress from "*Sehr geehrtes [deeply honored] Fräulein*" to "*Liebes Fräulein Felice;*" in another week she becomes "*Liebstes [dearest] Fräulein Felice;*" one more week passes and he addresses her using *du* (instead of the more formal *sie*):

> I am now going to ask you for a favor which sounds quite crazy...this is it: Write to me only once a week, so that your letter arrives on Sunday—for I cannot endure your daily letters....For instance, I answer one of your letters, then lie in bed in apparent calm, but my heart beats through my entire body and is conscious only of you. I belong to you; there is really no other way of expressing it, and that is not strong enough. But for this reason I don't want to know what you are wearing; it confuses me so much that I cannot deal with life; and that's why I don't want to know that you are well disposed toward me. If I did, how could I, fool that I am, go on sitting in my office, or here at home, instead of leaping onto a train with my eyes shut and opening them only when I am with you? Oh, there is a sad, sad reason for not doing so. To make it short: My health is only just good for myself alone, not good enough for marriage, let alone fatherhood. Yet when I read your letter, I feel I could overlook even what cannot possibly be overlooked.
>
> ...If only I had mailed Saturday's letter, in which I implored you never to write to me again, and in which

I gave a similar promise.... But is a peaceful solution possible now? Would it help if we wrote to each other only once a week? No, if my suffering could be cured by such means it would not be serious. And already I foresee that I shan't be able to endure even the Sunday letters. And so, to compensate for Saturday's lost opportunity, I ask you with what energy remains to me at the end of this letter: if we value our lives, let us abandon it all.

Did I think of signing myself Dein [yours]? No, nothing could be more false. I am forever fettered to myself. That's what I am, and that's what I must try to live with. (*LF*, 37)

It's all there in a nutshell: the charm offensive Kafka had commenced with the conquest of Felice as its goal; reflexive flight from that goal as soon as it is within reach; insistence on dealing with her and their future only on his terms; and self-denigration as a potent defense against intimacy that requires more than words. In the very next letter, Kafka is ecstatic over Felice's having accepted the principle of the *du*. And then, as though for the sake of good order, he inserts a bitter reminder of the limits on what they were to each other, as well as an intimation of his incapacity for marriage, and boundless, irremediable egocentricity.

Notwithstanding these warning signs, the struggle for Felice's heart was not long or unduly arduous. Eight weeks into the correspondence she had surrendered herself, addressing him as *Du*, permitting him to call her *Liebste, liebste* [dearest]. What was to be the next step? Middle-class Jews of the time in Berlin, Vienna, or Prague were not celebrated for their puritanism, and Felice was of an age to do exactly as she pleased. One may safely suppose that if they had found themselves alone in the right place she would have yielded her virginity without fuss. All that was required was for Kafka to go to Berlin or to arrange to meet at some halfway point and invite her, for instance, to his hotel room. To make the trip from Prague to Berlin and back to Prague over a short weekend was certainly tiring, but Kafka was not yet thirty, and men of that age and older have been known to undertake more punishing expeditions for the sake of taking their beloved in their arms. A few months later, Kafka spontaneously acknowledged the absurdity of his conduct. He imagined a conversation between Felice and one of her office colleagues:

> "Has this man [Kafka] actually been to Berlin once in the course of the past three months? He hasn't? And why not? He leaves Prague at noon on Saturday, or if that's not possible, then in the evening, spends Sunday in Berlin, and returns to Prague that night. It is a bit strenuous, but on the whole quite feasible. Why doesn't he do it?" Poor dearest, what would you say? (*LF*, 184)

Indeed, what could she say about this strange suitor? The question had some urgency since the 1912 Christmas vacation was approaching, and it was no longer strictly necessary to compress a visit to Berlin into a weekend. One might have expected that by now both Kafka and Felice would have taken it for granted that at last they would meet again, presumably in Berlin. It was not to be. The letters fly fast and thick, Kafka again complaining that her answers aren't arriving punctually. The growing tension in the correspondence so upset Felice that she asked Brod to intercede. He was successful, and the letters continued, alternating reproaches and apologies. Apparently, the subject of the Christmas vacation was brought into the open by Felice, and only in the second half of November. One can sense Kafka's consternation and alarm in his reply.

He acknowledges that the placement of the holidays is such that he "should have quite a reasonable Christmas vacation" and immediately points out his determination to use those days solely for his novel—*Amerika*—and perhaps *The Metamorphosis*, and that in any event he will lose one day of the vacation on account of his sister's wedding. And then he sails away from her and from their problem:

> Besides, I can't remember ever having traveled at Christmas; to traipse somewhere one day, traipse back the next: the futility of such an undertaking has always struck me as oppressive. Well, dearest, what about your vacation? Will you stay in Berlin in spite of your great need for relaxation? You wanted to go up into the mountains. Where? Any place where you would be accessible to me? You see, I was determined not to show my face until I had finished the novel, but I ask myself, *though only tonight*, would I be more worthy or at least less unworthy of you, dearest, after finishing it before? And is it not more important to allow my poor eyes to feast on you than to give free rein to my mania for writing during 6 consecutive days and nights? You tell me. I say for myself a big "Yes." (*LF*, 71–2)

We don't know how Felice answered this lukewarm and disingenuous proposal. Nothing more was said about Berlin until early December, when Kafka, in his best Jewish-mother manner, scolds her for staying in Berlin—there will be relatives, parties, and dancing, "and this is how you intend to rest?"—and lets it be known that his Christmas travels have become even more uncertain because his sister's wedding has been postponed until December 25, "thus threatening to disrupt the whole preceding Christmas vacation for me. But you too have visitors who might bar me from Berlin....Well, there is still time and therefore hope." (*LF*, 81) Then, one supposes because he is confident that the subject is safely behind him, he permits himself a moment of nostalgia:

> Dearest, I am getting very depressed about myself. Had I strung together the hours spent in writing to you and used them for a trip to Berlin, I should have been with you long ago, and could be looking into your eyes. And here I am, writing pages of absurdities as though life went on forever and ever and not a moment less. (*LF*, 87)

The hesitation waltz of wanting to go to Berlin and finding reasons not to go continues until he finally makes a visit the following March. In the lead-up to it, he writes, the day after Christmas: "when will I ever see you again? This summer? but why this summer, if I didn't see you at Christmas?" (*LF*, 125) He tells her that the question he had put to her "about coming to Berlin on the 1st [of April] was indeed a kind of joke even if not meant to be particularly funny...."(*LF*, 216) Finally, two weeks later, he puts to her "a point-blank question": would she be able to spare an hour on Easter Sunday or Monday to see him? Although he knows a number of people in Berlin, he assures her that he will not see them; at the hotel, he will stay close to the telephone and await her summons. And right away, having taken a step forward, he takes two steps back. Pursuing the theme, which will receive ample development in his subsequent letters, he informs her that he isn't a lover or marriage candidate she could reasonably accept:

> So the most important question is whether you consider it a good thing, and whether you are aware of the kind of visitor to expect. But I do not want to see your

relatives, dearest; I am not fit for that at present, and shall be even less so in Berlin; and when I say this I am not in the least considering that I have hardly a suit of clothes left in which to appear before you, even you. Not that this is of any importance, but one is tempted to avoid the important issues, which in any case you will see and hear—and take refuge in unimportant ones. So think it over carefully, Felice. You may not have the time, in which case no thought is required; everyone is bound to be home for Easter—your father, your brother, your sister from Dresden; your approaching move [to a new family apartment] will keep you busy; you will have to make arrangements for your trip to Frankfurt. In short, I shall understand perfectly if you don't have the time; I am not saying this on account of my own indecision, for I would then make an effort to come to Frankfurt in April, should you be in favor of it. (*LF*, 224)

The next day:

…something unpleasant, but very typical of me. I don't know whether I shall be able to come. It is still uncertain today, tomorrow may be definite.… But go on loving me despite this dithering. (*LF*, 224–5)

During the following night, he reminds her that the trip "depends above all on the view you take of it." (*LF*, 225) In the next letter, perhaps because she hadn't written and he had begun to think that she wouldn't want to see him, and will thus let him off the hook, he tells her that:

Strictly speaking the obstacle to my journey still exists and I'm afraid will continue to exist, but it has lost its significance as an *obstacle*; so, as far as that goes,

I could come. I just wanted to tell you this in haste dearest. No letter! (*LF*, 226)

That was on March 18. When he writes again, the letter from Felice agreeing to his visit has been received. It provokes an immediate attempt to throw cold water on the project:

I am going to Berlin for no other reason than to tell and show you—you who have been misled by my letters—who I really am. Shall I be able to make it clearer in person than I could in writing? In writing I failed, because I thwarted my purpose, consciously and unconsciously; but when I am actually there, little can be concealed, even if I make an effort to do so. Presence is irrefutable. (LF, 226)

As to whether he would actually appear, he hedges his bets:

Where can I meet you then on Sunday morning? However, should I still be prevented from coming, I would send a telegram on Saturday at the latest. (*LF*, 226)

Over the next three days, he sends conflicting signals about the business meeting he will perhaps be required to attend. The last communication in this vein is a three-word letter, postmarked on Good Friday: "Still undecided. Franz." (*LF*, 228) In the end, he does arrive in Berlin, and sends a letter by messenger from the hotel Askanische Hof, where he has always stayed:

But what has happened, Felice? You surely must have received my express letter on Friday in which I announced my arrival on Saturday night....And now I am in Berlin, and will have to leave again

this afternoon at 4 or 5; the hours are passing, and
no word from you....I am sitting at the Askanische
Hof—waiting. (*LF*, 228)

In all probability, the express letter was lost; it was not
included with the letters sold by Felice.

The brief meeting went well, if success or failure are to
be judged according to normal criteria; they agreed to meet
again in Berlin, in seven weeks, during the Whitsunday
weekend; and in the first letter written upon his return to
Prague he tells Felice that

> Since I left Berlin there have been few moments when
> I have not been entirely, and fundamentally and all-
> comprisingly yours....How close I came to you by my
> visit to Berlin! I breathe only through you. But you do
> not know me well enough, you dearest and best one,
> though it is incomprehensible to me how you could
> have closed your eyes to the things that were happening
> right next to you. Only out of kindness? And if that
> is possible, can't everything be possible? But I shall
> write in greater detail about that. (*LF*, 229–30)

In fact, his élan has diminished. A month will pass before
he writes another long-winded letter. But in short order
he brings into the open a subject that has been hinted at
once before:

> My one fear—surely nothing worse can either be
> said or listened to—is that I shall never be able to
> possess you. At best I would be confined, like an
> unthinkingly faithful dog, to kissing your casually
> proffered hand, which would not be a sign of love,
> but of the despair of the animal condemned to silence
> and eternal separation....

If this be true, Felice—and to me there seems to be no doubt—then surely I had good reason to part from you six months ago, and moreover good reason to fear any conventional bond with you, since the consequences of any such bond could only be the severing of my desire from the feeble forces that still sustain me—who am unfit for this earth—on this earth today. (*LF*, 233)

Two days later he writes to Brod and says that he has "sent his great confession to Berlin," and thinks he is "undermining the entire basis on which she previously used to live, happy and in tune with the whole world." (*L*, 95)

Having dropped this bombshell, Kafka reconsiders. He writes with the usual frequency, but the letters become uncharacteristically short. He receives a letter from Felice "unexpectedly." It puts him in an understandable state of nervousness, since he isn't sure that the confession has in fact already reached Berlin and caused the anticipated damage, so he tells her that he has no news, doubtless because he has told her too much. And then he adds the following note:

No, your express letter has just arrived. Dearest, to you who did not understand, nor could have understood that letter, my fears must seem idiotic; but they are horribly well-founded fears. (*LF*, 236)

It is hard to believe that Felice has not understood Kafka's allusion to his impotence. But it does not seem that she has been deeply affected. Very likely, she has confidence in her own power to attract and encourage—if only she is offered an opportunity. Her response must have been soothing, because for the moment nothing more is said on the subject; instead, Kafka informs her that he is working with a gardener in Nusle, a suburb of

Prague, "in the cool rain, in nothing but my shirt and trousers." (*LF*, 238) But it may be that he remembers her not having been discouraged by his first allusion to his limitations. That hint had come as we have seen at a time when for the first time he dared to address her using the *Du* form. If Felice is worried about Kafka's professed inability to "possess" her, she keeps her anxieties to herself, and, whether fortuitously or by design, makes a brilliant tactical move. She leaves for Frankfurt and Hanover to busy herself with the presentation her company is putting on at a trade fair. Not having her securely at her parents' apartment or at work, places he has already imagined and familiarized himself with, Kafka finds her instead shielded by her travel schedule from the barrage of his letters, postcards, and telegrams. For a change, he concentrates on keeping her. As for the intriguing question whether Kafka was in fact impotent, there is no reliable answer to be given. One can, however, reasonably suppose that his impotence was only intermittent, and that he required special circumstances, involving just the right quantity and combination of *strach* and *toucha* to be able to perform. The fact that he had frequented brothels and semiprofessional prostitutes does not prove anything. Brothels have made a specialty of catering to clients for whom sexual relations are difficult.

Underlying the backing and filling and the torment in Kafka's relationship with Felice is his belief that marriage was a duty he must assume and perhaps the only road to tranquil happiness, coupled with his fear of the aridity of an old bachelor's life. He had pondered all the sour horrors of the latter. For instance, in "Bachelor's Ill Luck," included in *Meditation*, we read:

It seems so dreadful to stay a bachelor, to become an old man struggling to keep one's dignity while begging for an invitation whenever one wants to spend an evening in company, to lie ill gazing for weeks into an empty room from the corner where one's bed is, always having to say good night at the front door, never to run up a stairway beside one's wife, to have only side doors in one's room leading into other people's living rooms, having to carry one's supper home in one's hand, having to admire other people's children and not even being allowed to go on saying 'I have none myself,' modeling oneself in appearance and behavior on one or two bachelors remembered from one's youth. (*CS*, 394–5)

Ironically, his belief that marriage and the foundation of a family are an indispensable part of a man's self-fulfillment, and a precondition to his happiness, finds its noblest—and most poignant—expression in a diary entry made in 1922, after he had broken with Milena. Although the breach was beyond repair, she continued to visit him sporadically. His physical and mental condition had touched bottom, and, although he would soon begin writing *The Castle*, for the moment he had no reason to think that he would be able to work again. "Without forebears," he wrote,

without marriage, without heirs, with a fierce longing for forebears, marriage, and heirs. They all of them stretch their hands to me: forebears, marriage, and heirs, but too far away for me.

There is an artificial, miserable substitute for everything, forebears, marriage, and heirs. Feverishly you contrive these substitutes, and if the fever has not already destroyed you, the hopelessness of the substitutes will. (*D*, 402–3)

In the absence of this profound conviction that marriage, however repellent, was necessary, it would be impossible to comprehend the five-year pursuit of Felice—the woman with the "[b]ony, empty face that wore its emptiness openly." (*D*, 207) Of her understanding of him, after two and a half years of sometimes daily correspondence, he could say, "F. in all likelihood understands nothing, which, because of our undeniable inner relationship, places her in a very special position." (*D*, 339) Of course, those words having been written, Kafka backpedaled and tried to moderate the harshness of his verdict:

Sometimes I thought she understood me without realizing it; for instance, the time she waited for me at the U-Bahn station—I had been longing for her unbearably, and in my passion to reach her as quickly as possible, almost ran past her, thinking she would be at the top of the stairs, and she took me quietly by the hand. (*D*, 339)

But the verdict was beyond alteration or appeal.

Over the May 11–12 Whitsunday holiday weekend, Kafka makes the scheduled second trip to Berlin. Its announcement is preceded by the usual tergiversations ("this is far from certain (I have a lot of work at the office)... I implore you not even to think of coming to meet me." (*LF*, 252) But he does arrive, and sees more of Felice than during the earlier visit; he meets her family. In the first letter upon his return to Prague, the happy suitor tells his beloved of the thought that filled his mind as he was packing his suitcase prior to leaving Berlin: "I cannot live without her, nor with her." (*LF*, 255) Two days later he comments on her family: "It was entirely in keeping with the situation; you are theirs, so they are big, you are not mine, so I was small... I must have made a very nasty impression on them." (*LF*, 257) Apparently, Felice requires that Kafka write her father, and Kafka assents. Weeks pass, and for once this inveterate letter writer cannot bring himself to comply. But he does come up with an idea: he will ask her father to advise him on the appropriateness of the marriage: "I shall ask him, provided he doesn't turn me down altogether, to name a physician he trusts, by whom I would then allow myself to be examined." (*LF*, 261) Examined to what end? Is it the impotence to which Kafka had already alluded? Something different? There are, Kafka tells her,

> certain difficulties for me which you are vaguely aware of, but which you don't take seriously enough, and which you wouldn't take seriously even if you were fully aware of them…for about ten years I have had this ever-growing feeling of not being in perfect health. (*LF*, 260)

Would the doctor understand the situation? Nothing is less certain, he writes on June 16; his own family doctor "with his stupid irresponsibility" is mystified. (*LF*, 269) But after telling her that what comes between her and him is the doctor, he finally asks the question that she doubtless wants to hear: "will you consider whether you wish to be my wife?" No sooner are those words out than he begins again to explain why it would be a mistake to marry him. She would lose Berlin, the work she enjoys, her friends,

> the prospect of marrying a decent, cheerful, healthy man, of having beautiful healthy children.…In place of these incalculable losses, you would gain a sick, weak, unsociable, taciturn, gloomy, stiff, almost helpless man who possibly has one virtue, which is that he loves you. (*LF*, 272)

In that long letter there was only one good thing he found he could say about himself: "All I possess are certain powers which, at a depth almost inaccessible under normal conditions, shape themselves into literature." (*LF*, 270)

She gives him the answer, "a little word on a postcard;" the word is yes, and Kafka's "knees begin to shake." (*LF*, 273) He wants to make sure that she has considered his objections to his suit point by point, and digested them. The yes should have been a no, and now he is prisoner of the contract he has proposed. On July 3—his thirtieth birthday—he tells his mother that Felice and he are engaged. She takes it calmly and makes a request to which he agrees: that he permit an investigative agency to gather information about the Bauer family. She needn't have worried that the marriage might be entered into hastily. Over the next eight weeks, with the single-minded purpose and passion of a fox biting off his own leg to free himself from a trap, Kafka will continue the work of self-demolition. He is determined to make Felice and her family agree that the marriage must not take place.

And, slowly, it becomes apparent that the central problem may not be sexual dysfunction but something akin to a writer's block. He has written nothing for five months. "The Stoker" and "The Judgment" had appeared in print in May and early June, but the powerful thrust that had carried him through the composition of those works and of *The Metamorphosis* had dissipated. Without writing, he tells her, "without this world in my head, this world straining to be released, I would have never dared to think of wanting to win you." (*LF*, 275) Needless to say, he throws in as well other reasons why she shouldn't marry him: they will be poor, he cannot abide company, he needs seclusion for writing—"not 'like a hermit,' but like the dead." (*LF*, 279) The letters he writes to her become shorter and he writes somewhat less frequently.

The period of vacations approaches. Felice decides to go away in August to Sylt, a small Frisian island that is the northernmost point in Germany. Kafka claims that he cannot take his holiday until September and suggests—perhaps not very seriously—that she come instead to Lake Garda, which is where he intends to spend his vacation in a sanatorium. The correspondence continues through the summer, with Kafka alternating between self-demolition and explanations of the impossibility of marriage and, when his anxieties are awakened, usually because she has been late in writing, something like renewed declarations of his love. He finally writes the letter to her father, effectively begging him to prevent the marriage. However, instead of sending it to Herr Bauer, he sends it to Felice, and it doesn't seem that she actually shows it to her parents. More likely she simply files it with the other missives from her strange lover. Then, on September 2, Kafka bolts. He points out that of the men he considers his blood relations, Grillparzer, Dostoevsky, Kleist, and Flaubert, only Dostoevsky married, and announces his departure first to Vienna on business and then, via Trieste and Venice, to the sanatorium in Riva, on Lake Garda. He warns her that he will not write to her "properly," and suggests that on his return "we can meet wherever you like; after all that time, we should be able to face each other calmly again." (*LF*, 317) In fact he does send a letter on September 16, from Venice. He tells her he is "prostrate," and concludes: "What am I to do, Felice? We shall have to part." (*LF*, 320). He will not write to her again until six weeks have passed.

One is baffled trying to imagine what Felice made of Kafka, his letters, and his odd attitudes and pretensions. Since there was no question in their relationship of sexual attraction so powerful that a young woman might be led to overlook or accept conduct as bizarre as Kafka's, a natural reaction on her part would have been put a halt to the courtship early on, perhaps after the tailspin he went into when she accepted his proposal, perhaps much earlier, for instance when he proved himself unable or unwilling to travel to Berlin over the Christmas holiday. What made her go on? Certainly Kafka was handsome, and could be charming and brilliant when he overcame his paralyzing shyness. She had met him under the roof of the respected Brod family and he held a secure position at the Insurance Institute. However, the income from that prestigious employment was unimpressive and the potential for its increase was limited. At best, he was an acceptable marriage candidate for this young woman, who could expect to be courted, as Kafka himself put it, by cheerful and decent men. He was entitled to write letters to her and to receive answers, provided his letters remained conventional, having as their presumed object matrimony. Instead, she found herself involved in epistolary exchanges with a maniac.

A possible explanation of her conduct is that, with or without the influence of Brod, she had recognized that Kafka was a genius as well as a species of madman. Or perhaps she simply succumbed to the magical power of his letters. Whatever the reason, Felice did not give up. In a letter dated October 29 Kafka told her: "My longing for you is such that it presses on my breast like tears that cannot be wept." (*LF*, 321) Instead of recoiling at what might have seemed conclusive proof of Kafka's imbalance, she dispatched Grete Bloch (1892–1944?) to repair the relationship. This should not have been an easy undertaking, Kafka's feelings being a maelstrom of self-contradictions. Writing toward the end of September from the sanatorium in Riva—where he had fallen in love with a Christian Swiss girl "and had lived almost entirely within the sphere of her influence" (*D*, 232)—he told Max Brod that

> every honeymoon couple, whether or not I put myself
> in their place, is a repulsive sight to me, and when I

want to disgust myself I have only to imagine placing
my arm around a woman's waist.

Two sentences later he beat a partial retreat, and repeats
what he had once written Felice: "I cannot live with her
[Felice] and I cannot live without her." (*L*, 102).

Grete was no ordinary emissary. Five years younger than
Felice, prettier than she, Grete was a native of Berlin. Unlike
Felice, she had graduated from a business school, and
afterward had worked as a shorthand typist, first in Berlin,
then in Vienna, and then again in Berlin. The women's
friendship, a recent one—probably dating from the summer
of 1913—endured until at least 1935, when Grete gave
Felice the letters Kafka had written to her.

As bidden, Grete went to Prague, met Kafka, and, in
the course of the months to come, vindicated Felice's
confidence in her efficiency. An unprogrammed result of
Grete's efforts was that Kafka wrote to her as well. The
correspondence begins with Kafka's letter on November
1, and goes strong for a year into the fall of 1914. Though
they bear witness to a rapidly established affectionate
camaraderie, these are not love letters. There are no
declarations of love; Kafka addresses Grete as "*gnädiges
[gracious] Fräulein*" or "*liebes Fräulein;*" he never uses the
du form. It is impossible, on the other hand, to resist the
impression that Kafka enjoyed writing to Grete more than
he had ever enjoyed writing to Felice: Grete must have
been the more lively and more intelligent correspondent. A
curious fiction hangs over Kafka's relationship with Grete.
Sixteen years after his death, at a time when she was living
in Italy, Grete alleged in a letter to a friend in Israel that
she had borne Kafka's son, who had died suddenly at the
age of seven in Munich. There is not a shred of evidence
in any of Kafka's correspondence or in his diary, or in

Brod's recollections, to support Grete's claim, which is on its face incredible given Kafka's character and everything that is known of his whereabouts and occupations. It is best ascribed to the immense stress to which Grete had become subject as a Jewish woman of German nationality living in fascist Italy. She was deported from Italy and murdered by the Germans, but the date of her death is not certain.

As with Kafka's letters to Felice, his letters to Grete soon reach an apogee of nosiness. A little over a month following their meeting, he tells her, after she mentions Felice's trouble with her teeth, that this is one of "the most repulsive ailments, which I can overlook only in people most dear to me, and then only just..." (*LF*, 327) Not unnaturally, Grete read his letter as expressing annoyance with her account. Two letters later, Kafka hastens to reassure her:

> I was extremely interested, there was nothing I would rather have listened to; for my liking, you told me far too little; the abscess under the bridge, the piecemeal breaking-off of the bridge, I should like to have heard about that with every detail and even asked F. about it in Berlin. (*LF*, 330)

The interest he took in Grete's own life seems sometimes fraternal, as when he counsels her on the importance of leaving Vienna, a deadening city in his opinion, and returning to Berlin. He concerns himself with her cultural development, sending her books, commenting on them, and encouraging her to become interested in Franz Grillparzer, an Austrian writer with whom he felt a particular kinship. But in no time solicitude turns into the need to control. "By the way, how do you spend your Sundays," he asks, after your exertions during the week? Is it wise to exert yourself in this way? Will you be able to keep it up for long? What was the illness you told me about the other day? The time you spent on your last letter was probably snatched from your lunch hour; that is as wrong as it is kind. But I won't say any more, for I am now altogether more indebted to you than to any other human being. (*LF*, 345)

Or,

With whom do you play the piano, and go on excursions in the mountains? (*LF*, 347)

He returns to the subject of teeth—Grete's, Felice's, and his own—in astonishing detail in a letter written shortly before the reception at the Bauer family apartment on June 1, 1914, when his engagement to Felice became official. Responding to Grete's having told him that she was suffering from a toothache, he writes:

So far, however, I may not have suffered the very direst form of toothache, and I read about it in your letter with the utter perplexity of a schoolboy. How, in fact, do you attend to your teeth? Do you brush them after each meal? (Alas, I am now addressing the lady who, thanks to a toothache, disregards politeness and formality.) What do the infernal dentists say? Once in their hands, one has to taste the misery to the bitter end. I think F., with practically an entire mouthful of gold-capped teeth, has relatively little trouble. To tell the truth, this gleaming gold (a really hellish luster for this inappropriate spot) so scared me at first that I had to lower my eyes at the sight of F.'s teeth and the grayish yellow porcelain. After a time, whenever I could, I glanced at it on purpose so as not to forget it, to torment myself, and finally to convince myself that all this is really true. In a thoughtless moment I even asked F. if it didn't embarrass her. Of course, it didn't—fortunately. But now I have become almost entirely reconciled, and not merely from habit (in fact I hadn't the time to acquire a visual habit). I now no longer wish these gold teeth gone, but that is not quite the right expression, for I actually never did wish them gone. It's rather that they now strike me as almost becoming, most suitable, and—this is not unimportant—a very definite, genial, ever-present, visually undeniable human blemish which brings me perhaps closer to F. than could a healthy set of teeth, also horrible in its way. (*LF*, 405–6)

That is Kafka at his worst, overstepping all barriers of good manners, and garrulously disloyal to Felice. Two letters later, he offers Grete advice on dental hygiene.

If the deterioration of the teeth wasn't actually due to inadequate care, then it was due, as with me, to eating meat...tiny shreds of meat between the teeth produce germs of decay and fermentation no less than a dead rat squashed between two stones.

Meat is the one thing that is so stringy that it can be removed only with great difficulty, and even then not at once and not completely, unless one's teeth are like those of a beast of prey—pointed, set wide apart, designed for the purpose of tearing meat to shreds. (*LF*, 408)

Meanwhile it has become apparent that Grete, busy as she is with their correspondence, is accomplishing her mission. On November 8 and 9, Kafka is in Berlin; the trip "was largely [Grete's] doing" and unsatisfactory. He sees Felice only during a short walk they took in the Tiergarten. But at the end of December, contacts resume: in a letter written over a period of three days, December 29, 1913, to January 2, 1914, Kafka asks her once again to marry him, but not before confessing. At the sanatorium in Riva, he tells her, "I fell in love with a girl, a child, about eighteen years old; she is Swiss, but lives in Italy near Genoa, thus by blood as alien to me as can be; still immature but remarkable and despite her illness a real person with great depth." He assures her, however, that "[w]ith my departure it was all over." (*LF*, 335)

Felice doesn't give a real answer; she sends a postcard. On February 9, in reply to the postcard, he writes again, pleading for a letter. None is received, and on February 28, Kafka again goes to Berlin to see her, returning the next day to Prague. Reporting to Grete in a postcard from Dresden, he writes: "It couldn't have been worse. The next thing will be impalement." (*LF*, 352) Nothing quite so dreadful happens. The month and a half that follow are given over to two campaigns, one to persuade Grete to visit him in Prague, the other to reestablish contact with Felice. In the Tiergarten she had set out, quite sensibly, the reasons for which she would not marry him. He summarized them in a letter to Grete:

> F. quite likes me, but in her opinion this is not enough for marriage, for this particular marriage; she has insurmountable fears about a joint future; she might not be able to put up with my idiosyncrasies; she might not be able to forgo Berlin; she is afraid of having to dispense with nice clothes, of traveling third class, sitting in cheaper seats in the theater...(*LF*, 353)

They aren't very different from the objections to their marriage with which he had bombarded her. Nevertheless, he enlists his mother in the campaign to bring Felice around and even writes to her parents, asking them to let him know whether their daughter isn't writing because she is ill. The badgering is relentless, by letter and, surprisingly, by telephone, and it comes on top of a blow Felice and her parents had just suffered. The only son, Ferry, had gotten into serious financial difficulties that obliged him to emigrate to America. Finally, Felice's defenses are worn down. With her permission, Kafka comes to Berlin in April, at Easter, and they became unofficially engaged. She agrees to marry him in September. On April 14 he writes that "I have never at any time taken a step which has left me as firmly convinced of having done the right and absolutely necessary thing…" (*LF*, 384)

All the while, Kafka has been corresponding assiduously with Grete. He announces to her the engagement the day of his return to Prague, assures her that nothing has changed in his relationship with her, refuses to return her letters, and presses her to send him photographs of her, which she sends. More remarkably, he urges her to come to Prague when Felice will be there to make courtesy visits and look at apartments, and suggests that she move to Prague and live in Felice's and his apartment for at least six months after the marriage. There is a tone of enjoyment and friendly banter in his letters to Grete utterly missing from those to his fiancée. Felice does come to Prague as scheduled, although without Grete, and an apartment is duly selected. But dealing with her over their future installation and, one supposes, having a foretaste of what married life will be like, puts him into a state of cold fury. "Really, Felice?" he writes,

Time is passing too swiftly for you? Already the end of May? Already? Well, here I am holding the key; if you

like, I'll wind back the time. To which month during
the past two years shall I wind it back? Tell me exactly!
(*LF*, 416)

The next event is the official engagement, which takes
place in Berlin, with a reception on June 1 at the Bauer
family apartment. Kafka's parents and Ottla are present,
as well as Grete, to whom Kafka wrote: "Just hurry, and
get to F., to whom I have divulged nothing, regardless of
your dress, don't try to improve it no matter what it's like,
it will be viewed with the, yes, with the most affectionate
eyes." (*LF*, 418)

Kafka may have believed that he had done the right and
absolutely necessary thing by becoming engaged to Felice,
but one would never know it from the premonitory notation
in his diary after his return to Prague, on June 6, in which
he reports that at the reception in the Bauers' apartment
he felt he had been tied hand and foot like a criminal. (*D*,
275) In the weeks that follow, Kafka writes regularly to
Grete. No letters to Felice have been preserved.

On July 1, he informs Grete breezily that he is going to
Berlin, or rather will be going on vacation via Berlin, and
asks whether she will be in Berlin. Grete had in the interim
moved to Berlin from Vienna. A draft of a letter from Grete,
presumably in reply, survives. It is full of reproach and
informs him that "I had only a brief word with F. After
all these letters, I hardly dare to look her in the eye." (*LF*,
431) Does Kafka know what to expect in Berlin? There is
no hint of it except perhaps in his reply to Grete, written
on July 3, his thirty-first birthday, in which he claims to
have "convinced" her—presumably of his unsuitability for
Felice—and mentions having received in addition to her
own letter one that was "extremely unpleasant." Perhaps
that was a letter from Felice, with a bill of particulars of the
charges that would be leveled against him. The meeting

takes place in Berlin on July 12, at the Askanische Hof. Present in addition to Kafka and Felice are Grete and Felice's sister, Erna. It may be that Kafka's new friend, Dr. Ernst Weiss (1882–1940), a physician and novelist who dislikes Felice, and is in Berlin at the time, is present as well.

What took place at the hotel is not clear, but it would seem that Kafka stood convicted. But of what crime? Apparently one cobbled together with excerpts from his letters to Grete, which Grete had allowed her to read. That Kafka was gallant and seductive in those letters is certain. Perhaps that was enough. Perhaps the objections to the feasibility of the marriage he had voiced, none of which could have seemed new to Felice since he had previously rehearsed them for her, also weighed in the judgment. Perhaps the truth was that she was no more convinced than he that the marriage should take place. In his diary, Kafka wrote of "the tribunal in the hotel," F.'s saying to him "very studied, hostile things she had been saving up," the visit to the parents who were sympathetic, as was Erna, and "Fräulein Bl.[och]'s apparent guilt." (*D*, 293) He had more to say about Grete's role in a letter to her written the following October: "At the Askanische Hof you sat in judgment over me—it was horrible for you, for me, for everyone—but it only appeared to be so; in fact I was sitting there in your place, which to this day I have not left." (*LF*, 436) Two days after later, Kafka left for the two-week vacation he had previously planned with Weiss and Weiss's mistress, Rahel Sansara, in the Baltic resorts of Travemünde and Marielyst. He returned to Prague at the end of July. On August 2, Germany declared war on Russia.

This should have been the ending of Kafka's involvement with Felice. That they had almost nothing in common was apparent to Kafka even as he was writing his most ardent letters. Her own reluctance can only be inferred, except, as we have seen, when her objections were brought into the open in Kafka's letter to Grete of March 1914, in which he quoted what Felice had told him in the Tiergarten. But a strange fatality pushed them forward. In October 1914, with the engagement dissolved, Grete and Felice wrote to him. He answered both letters, the letter to Felice, extraordinarily long even by Kafka's standards, being the clearest statement of what divided them. It was the unresolved conflict between her yearning for a normal bourgeois household and a normal bourgeois life, and his absolute need to subordinate everything to his work. (*LF*, 436–441) Nevertheless, in January 1915, they meet in Bodenbach, a town on the River Elbe on the Czech side of the border with Germany. The meeting is yet another disaster. He finds that they are unchanged, she in her demands, he in his concept of a life constrained only by the demands of his work.

> I yield not a particle of my demand for a fantastic life arranged solely in the interest of my work; she, indifferent to every mute request, wants the average: a comfortable home, an interest on my part in the factory, good food, bed at eleven, central heating… (*D*, 328)

She corrects his German when he speaks to the waiter, sets his watch right to the minute, calls his elder sisters shallow, and doesn't ask for news of his beloved Ottla. Worse yet, she lies on the sofa with her eyes closed while he reads to her, perking up only when he reads the "Before the Law" section from *Trial*.

The correspondence continues in a desultory fashion, with Kafka's letters demonstrating a new wariness. Toward the end of May, there is another meeting with Felice, this time in the mountains on the Czech side of the Elbe. Improbable though it may seem, Grete is in attendance, and perhaps due to her mediation they have a good time. Kafka returns to

Prague ecstatic, and writes that he has sought memories of F. and her room among the lilacs. (*LF*, 455) A playful tone creeps into his letters: he adopts the convention of referring to himself as F.'s bridegroom. But they are stretching their luck: a meeting with Felice alone in Karlsbad in June is not a success. He writes to her, but it as though he wanted to keep her at bay. At the beginning of December he tells her "It would be nice to meet; nevertheless we should not do so.... I could bring you nothing but disappointments, monster of insomnia and headaches that I am." (*LF*, 459) In March 1916 (the date uncertain) he writes a letter remarkable for its lucid diagnosis of what had gone wrong between them. First, there is her insistence on "keeping me" in Prague, "although you ought to have realized that it was precisely the office that would lead to my—thus our—eventual ruin." (*LF*, 462)

Presumably, practical young woman that she is, Felice doesn't want him to give up the secure position at the Institute. But, the way of life she instinctively chooses at every opportunity clashes with his. He writes:

> we went to buy furniture in Berlin for an official in Prague. Heavy furniture which looked as if, once in position, it could never be removed. Its very solidity is what you appreciated most. The sideboard in a particular—a perfect tombstone, or a memorial to the life of a Prague official—oppressed me profoundly. If during our visit to the furniture store a funeral bell had begun tolling in the distance, it wouldn't have been inappropriate. (*LF*, 462)

So it continues until, in May 1916, Kafka goes on business to Marienbad and finds it "unbelievably beautiful." (*LF*, 469) He suggests to Felice that she join him there, a suggestion all the more practical in that it doesn't require them to deal with wartime passport restrictions. They spend ten days there together, July 3–13, 1916, during which they both write to Felice's mother announcing their new engagement. On July 13, they visit Kafka's mother in Franzensbad, where she is spending the summer. The following day, Felice returns to Berlin and Kafka to Marienbad. Writing to Brod, Kafka tells him that after

> a series of frightful days, spawned in even more frightful nights...the cords with which I was trussed were at last somewhat loosened; I straightened out somewhat while she, who had constantly been holding out her hands to help but reaching only into an utter void, helped again and we arrived at a human relationship of a kind I had so far never known and which came very near in its meaningfulness to the relationship we had achieved at the best periods of our correspondence.... I saw the look of trustfulness in a woman's eyes, and I could not fail to respond. (*L*, 117)

That positive view of what has happened doesn't blind Kafka to the reality of their past, or the part played in it by his nature, or to what may still be in store for them. He continues his letter:

> Much has been torn open that I wanted to shield forever (I am not speaking of anything in particular but of the whole); and through this rent will come, I know, enough unhappiness for more than a lifetime, but this unhappiness is nothing summoned up, but rather imposed. I have no right to shirk it, especially since, if what is happening were not happening, I would of my own accord make it happen, simply to

have her turn that look upon me. I did not really know her up to now. Aside from other doubts, last time I was hampered by an actual fear of the reality of this girl behind the letters. When she came toward me in the big room to receive the engagement kiss, a shudder ran through me. The engagement trip with my parents was sheer agony for me, every step of the way. I have never feared anything so much as being alone with F. before the wedding. Now all that has changed and is good. (*L*, 117–8)

They agree to get married soon after the end of the war. Renting a small apartment in a Berlin suburb, each will "assume economic responsibilities for himself." (*L*, 117) In Kafka's case, that means supporting himself by writing.

The war, of course, drags on pitilessly. They quarrel in November in Munich, where she attends a reading of *In the Penal Colony* that Kafka gives before an apathetic if not hostile audience. No subsequent letters to Felice written in the first eight months of 1917 have survived, and there are no entries concerning her in the diaries. However, we have Brod's recollections of Kafka and Felice as fiancés during that summer:

a flat was taken for the young couple, furniture was bought, and Franz had already begun the conventional round of calls on relatives and acquaintances and even went to Hungary, to Arad, with F., to pay a visit to her sister....Comically enough, the pair of them even paid me a formal call, on July 9, 1917—the sight of the two, both rather embarrassed, above all Franz, wearing an unaccustomed high stiff collar, had something moving in it, and at the same time something horrible. (*B*, 157)

Then, at about five in the morning on August 10, Kafka suffered the first serious hemorrhage. Badgered by Brod, in September he twice consulted a lung specialist, and was told he had catarrh of the lungs with a risk of tuberculosis. A three months' leave was mandated along with a rest cure, preferably in the south, or, if that was not practicable, in the countryside. As luck had it, Ottla had taken over the management of a small property in Zürau, a tiny village some sixty miles from Prague, belonging to their sister Elli's husband, Karl Hermann. Kafka arranged to stay with her, and remained until April 18, 1918. Before leaving Prague, he wrote Felice that he had tuberculosis of both lungs, but had not yet told his parents. Three weeks later, he wrote again, from Zürau, explaining the struggle within him of the good part, which had hoped it would be allowed to have her, with the evil part, that wanted to prevent it. For the good part, "the loss of blood was too great." The illness wasn't necessarily tuberculosis, "but rather a sign of my general bankruptcy.... The blood issues not from the lung, but from a decisive stab delivered by one of the combatants." He concluded by telling her that he would never be well again. (*LF*, 545–6)

Kafka had understood at once the implications of his illness for the engagement for which, and against which, he had fought so long and so hard: he had been set free. After the second visit to the specialist, he wrote in his diary:

You have a chance, as far as it at all possible, to make a new beginning. Don't throw it away.... If the infection in your lungs is only a symbol, as you say, a symbol of the infection whose inflammation is called F. and whose depth is its deep justification; if this is so then the medical advice (light, air, sun, rest) is also a symbol. Lay hold of this symbol.

> O wonderful moment, masterful version, garden
> gone to seed. You turn the corner as you leave the
> house and the goddess of luck rushes towards you
> down the garden path. (*D*, 383)

In the same vein, but more explicitly, he also wrote to Brod in mid-September:

> my brain and lungs came to an agreement without
> my knowledge. "Things can't go on this way," said
> the brain, and after five years the lungs said that they
> were ready to help. (*L*, 138)

Having traveled thirty hours, according to Kafka's diary, Felice came to see him in Zürau on September 20 and 21. "As I see it," he wrote, "suffering the utmost misery, and the guilt is essentially mine." (*D*, 385) The visit changed nothing. On October 8, he noted that he had received a letter of complaint from her, and that "G. B. [Grete Bloch] threatens me with writing a letter." Felice came to see him once more, on December 25–27, in Prague. Although Kafka was reduced to tears, he held firm. (*B*, 166–7) The engagement was officially broken during this visit, with Kafka's illness given out as the reason. In 1919, Felice married a Berlin businessman. A little over a year later, when she was pregnant with her second child, Kafka wrote to Brod:

> I feel for F. the love that an unsuccessful general has
> for the city he could not take, but which "nevertheless"
> became something great—a happy mother of two.
> (*L*, 247)

There was a bittersweet intermezzo between Kafka's five-year struggle to conquer Felice and to be set free of her and the wondrous year in which he won and lost the heart of Milena. In late January or early February 1919, at the Pension Stüdl in the Bohemian mountain village of Schelesen, where Kafka had gone on medical leave to recuperate from a bout first with Spanish influenza and then with double pneumonia, he met Julie Wohryzek, the twenty-two-year-old daughter of a shoemaker and synagogue custodian, and herself a milliner. He described her in a letter to Brod, written in Schelesen:

> The Jewish element is a young woman, only, it is to be hoped, slightly ill.... Not Jewish and yet not not-Jewish, not German and yet not not-German, crazy about the movies, about operettas and comedies, wears face powder and veils, possesses an inexhaustible and nonstop store of the brashest Yiddish expressions, in general very ignorant, more cheerful than sad—that is about what she is like. If one wanted to classify her racially, one would have to say that she belonged to the race of shopgirls. (*L*, 213)

We learn more about Julie, and about Kafka's relationship with her, from a surprising letter he wrote to her sister, with whom he had "only a brief acquaintanceship." (*L*, 215) Nonetheless, he does not hesitate to tell her that she—the elder sister—seems to him

> basically kind, also controlled and deliberate, though somewhat too melancholic, a trifle dissatisfied, a trifle hapless, and because of these very qualities capable of an understanding that goes beyond the immediate sphere of your life and experience. (*L*, 215)

After this introduction, which must have made the sister gulp, he proceeded to explain that at the beginning he and Julie

laughed continually whenever we met each other, at
meals, while walking, while sitting opposite each other.
On the whole the laughter was not pleasant; it had no
apparent reason, was painful, shameful. (*L*, 215)

One supposes the reason was sudden sexual attraction. But
they remained "magnificently brave," so that he "truly
suffered to the full the anguish of all animal nature...."
(*L*, 216) They established between them that

I regarded marriage and children as one of the desirable things on earth in a certain sense, but I could
not possibly marry. (*L*, 216)

So they parted: chaste and without having progressed to
the point of saying *du* to each other.

But, when they returned to Prague, they "flew to each
other as if driven." (*L*, 217) They walked in the deep woods
and in Prague streets, they went swimming, and, whether
Kafka admitted it to himself or not, they were having a good
time. Whereupon, incorrigibly, he insisted on marriage.
The engagement to Julie ran into furious opposition from
his father. The butcher's son did not want to be disgraced by
his only son's bringing into the family the daughter of the
synagogue shammes. Kafka was not deterred, but he threw
his words back at him in the *Letter*, which he composed in
November of that year:

You said to me something like this: "She probably put
on a fancy blouse, something these Prague Jewesses
are good at, and right away, of course, you decided
to marry her. And that as fast as possible, in a week,
tomorrow, today. I can't understand you: after all
you're a grown man, you live in the city, and you don't
know what to do but marry the first girl who comes

along. Isn't there anything else you can do? If you're frightened, I'll go with you." (*S*, 159)

If that is indeed how his father taunted him, the scene was, as we shall see, magnificently and eerily prefigured, in yet another instance of life imitating art, by the father's explosion on the subject of the son's fiancée in "The Judgment."

The marriage plan collapsed anyway, after the banns had been published. Two days before the wedding, the apartment that Kafka thought he had secured—no mean task given the postwar housing shortage in Prague— "slipped though our fingers." (*L*, 219) In the circumstances, Kafka told the sister, who thought the relationship should end, that he was willing to let Julie go either if she had a "halfway reasonable prospect of… marrying, and fairly soon, some good man whom she is willing to accept, and living with him as purely and decently as is possible for ordinary people," or if it turned out that after all that she was not content to continue their existing relationship outside marriage, but with "love and fidelity." (*L*, 219) The result of these developments was that when the correspondence with Milena commenced in the spring of 1920, Kafka was still engaged to Julie and, in fact, had made plans to meet her for a short holiday in Karlsbad.

"She is a living fire," he wrote to Brod, "of a kind I have never seen before, a fire moreover that in spite of everything burns only for him." (*L*, 237) The living fire was Milena Jesenská. The man for whom Kafka thought her flame burned was her husband, Ernst Polak. Milena was part of Prague's Czech-speaking, ethnic Czech elite. A successful oral surgeon and professor at the Charles University in Prague, her father was a hard-line nationalist and anti-Semite. Milena had the reputation of having been wild as an adolescent and having experimented with drugs and probably sex. Polak, a Prague Jew ten years older than Milena, was a cultivated intellectual who worked at a bank but spent his leisure hours with writers at the Café Arco, the principal meeting place of Prague's literati. Milena and he had had an affair which, coming on top of Milena's other misconduct, so outraged her father that he had her committed to a hospital for the mentally ill. Released when she attained majority, she married Polak, moved with him to Vienna, and lived with him there in an "open marriage" that was to prove for her a source of considerable suffering. The father gave her little money.

Polak worked for the parent company of the bank at which he had been employed in Prague, but his earnings could not support both Milena and the liaisons with other women. The result was that Milena had to find ways to round out the couple's finances. She turned to journalism, writing for Czech periodicals in Prague, in particular *Tribuna*. In addition, she translated from German to Czech. Kafka had met her in Prague, and knew Polak as a fixture of the literary scene. But the immediate impetus for their correspondence came from the translation she was preparing of the "The Stoker," which had been published as a stand-alone story in 1913 by Kurt Wolff in his collection "Der Jüngste Tag." She seems to have written to Kafka about it in November 1919, and then again, in April 1920. As we have seen, he was at the time on medical leave in Merano. Very quickly, already in his third letter to her, a tone of intimacy became established. She must have told him that she wasn't well because, in reply, he writes:

So it's the lung. I've been turning it over in my mind all day long, unable to think of anything else. Not that it alarms me; probably one may hope—you seem to indicate as much—you have a mild case, and even

full-fledged pulmonary disease (half of western Europe
has more or less deficient lungs), as I have known in
myself for three years, has brought me more good
things than bad. (*LM*, 5)

From there he goes on to tell her in detail about his first
hemorrhage. That having been disposed of, he tells her
that she may indeed write to him in Czech, and that he
wants her to do so, because "after all, you belong to that
language, because only there can Milena be found in her
entirety." She had asked about his engagement. He replies
that he has been engaged three times (twice to the same
girl), and that while the engagements to the first girl, Felice,
are over, the engagement to Julie, "is still alive though
without any prospect of marriage..." (*LM*, 8) Throughout
the correspondence he will refer to Julie as the "girl," save
once, when he gives Milena her name and address so that
she may write her. Two letters later, in reply to her asking
whether he is a Jew, comes the first of a series of Kafka's
remarkable attempts to define for her the consequences of
being a Jew. "Their insecure position," he tells her,

insecure within themselves, insecure among people,
would above all explain why Jews believe they possess only whatever they hold in their hands or grip
between their teeth, that furthermore only tangible
possessions give them a right to live, and that finally
they will never again acquire what once they have
lost....Jews are threatened by dangers from the most
improbable sides, or, to be more precise, let's leave
the dangers aside and say: "They are threatened by
threats." (*LM*, 20)

By the end of May, she has asked him to come to Vienna.
He first tells her that he doesn't want to and besides can't—

he couldn't stand the mental stress. He is spiritually ill, the lung disease being "but an overflowing of my spiritual disease" linked to his guilt about the suffering he had inflicted on Felice. (*LM*, 22–3) Then he confesses the immediate problem: he has told Julie that he will meet her for a brief holiday in Karlsbad. Later that day he changes his mind: "I wired Prague to say that I cannot come to Karlsbad...that's how I play with a real live human being." (*LM*, 25) But even so he won't go to Vienna. When he writes on June 1, he has received two letters from Milena. Replying, he tells her that it is his sleepless brain that answers. Since he can't think of anything to write, he is just walking around between the lines

> underneath the light of your eyes, in the breath of your mouth like in some beautiful happy day, which stays beautiful and happy even if my head is sick, tired, and I have to leave Monday via Munich. (*LM*, 26)

Going to Prague via Munich precludes stopping in Vienna. Whether he will after all come to Vienna, and if so when that might be, become subjects of a debate, reminiscent of the back-and-forth about going to Berlin to see Felice, that continues in the correspondence until the visit finally takes place, over a four-day period at the end of June.

In the meantime, the progress to intimacy accelerates. When he writes to her twice on June 12, he uses *du*, the mode of address she has initiated. In a letter sent the previous day, he had said *du* only once; it is a sly maneuver: "I take the letter out of the envelope, here it is: Please say it once more—not always, I don't wish it at all—say *Du* to me once again." (*LM*, 41) In the second letter he tells her "*you belong to me*, even if I should never see you again." (*LM*, 43) One hears the disturbing echo of the first time he said *du* to Felice and told her "I belong to you." He

wants Milena to leave Vienna, to leave her husband at least
for some period of time. He will give her the necessary
funds, but isn't suggesting that they live together. His
concern for Ernst Polak surges, partially in response to
the news—which he gives her—of the suicide of a young
Prague journalist, Joseph Reiner, who had recently killed
himself after discovering his wife's affair with another
Prague figure we have already encountered, Willy Haas.
Reiner had been married to a friend of Milena's. Moreover,
he is haunted by the "Jewish question," the image of the
Jew as the predator whose prey is Christian girls. Is that
what he is doing? Kafka's letters at this time border on folly.
The same must have been true of Milena's. "You see," he
wrote to her,

> the peaceful letters are the ones that make me happy
> (understand, Milena, my age, the fact that I am used
> up, and above all my fear, and understand your youth,
> your vivacity, your courage....). But whenever these
> other letters come, Milena, even though they are
> basically more auspicious than the first ones (although
> on account of my weakness it takes me days to pen-
> etrate to their happiness)—these letters that begin
> with exclamations (and after all, I am so far away), and
> which end with I don't know what terrible things, then,
> Milena, I literally start to shake as if under an alarm
> bell; I am unable to read them and naturally I read
> them anyway, the way an animal dying of thirst drinks,
> and with that comes fear and more fear; I look for a
> piece of furniture to crawl under; trembling, totally
> unaware of the world, I pray you might fly back out
> the window the way you came storming in inside your
> letter. After all, I can't keep a storm in my room; in
> these letters you undoubtedly have the magnificent
> head of Medusa, the snakes of terror are quivering

about your head so wildly, while the snakes of fear quiver even more wildly about my own. (*LM*, 45)

The happiness during the visit to Vienna, when it finally takes place, is the high-water mark in their relationship. What happened can be gleaned from a letter that Milena wrote to Max Brod early in 1921, after the rupture between Kafka and her had become complete. She told Brod that she had understood "down to my deepest nerve" Kafka's fear. Fear of what? Of the flesh, as foreshadowed in the anecdote concerning the shopgirl he had recounted to Milena in order to explain the twin forces of fear and desire. "This fear doesn't just apply to me," she wrote,

it relates to everything that is shamelessly alive, also to the flesh, for example. Flesh is too uncovered; he can't stand the sight of it. This is what I was able to dispel back then [in Vienna]. Whenever he sensed this fear, he would look me in the eye, and we would wait a while, as if our feet hurt or we had to catch our breath, and after a moment it would pass. This didn't require the slightest effort, everything was simple and clear, I dragged him over the hills behind Vienna, I went on ahead since he was walking slowly, he came trudging on behind me, and if I close my eyes I can still see his white shirt and his sunburned neck and how he was straining. He kept hiking the whole day, uphill, downhill, in the sun; he didn't cough once, he ate an enormous amount and slept like a bagpipe; he was simply healthy, and during those days his disease was like a slight cold. Had I gone to Prague with him back then, I would have remained the person I was for him at the time. But I was also planted with two feet here, infinitely firmly in the ground; I was incapable of leaving my husband, and perhaps I was too much

of a woman to have the strength to subject myself to
a life that I knew would demand the most rigorous
asceticism for the rest of my days. (*LM*, 248)

That was Vienna. In Prague, Kafka returns to complications of day-to-day reality, for some of which he has
himself to blame. He sees Julie; she is distraught, as might
have been expected, and he foolishly agrees that she may
write to Milena. He also agrees to see her the next day, and
"to go off with her somewhere in the afternoon." (*LM*, 69)
At times he wants to return to Vienna; however, there are
obstacles. He isn't even certain that Milena wishes him
to come. Contacts with her Czech women friends are
confusing and unsatisfactory and provoke antagonisms.
There are also more contacts with Julie and more of Kafka's
egregious indiscretions. When Julie asks for the address of
Milena's husband, he gives it to her. He resists Milena's
apparent wish to see him in Prague:

You write you might come to Prague next month. I
almost feel like saying: Don't come. Leave me the
hope that you'll come *immediately* if I should ever
be in urgent need...right now it would be better if
you didn't come, since you'd only have to leave again.
(*LM*, 95)

His health is deteriorating. His doctor finds him in much
the same shape as before he had left for Merano. The lesion
at the top of the left lung isn't healing. "He considers the
result bleak..." (*LM*, 85) Kafka is consumed by jealousy of
Polak, disturbed about the plans he gets wind of, according
to which Polak might move to Paris or Heidelberg. When
the subject of Milena's visit to Prague comes up again,
he writes—unforgivably—that he doesn't wish her to be
"misled by the days in Vienna. Isn't it possible that we owed

something to your unconscious hope of being able to see him [Polak] again in the evening?" (*LM*, 92) They are in touch about Milena's translations of two of his stories, "Bachelor's Ill Luck," and "Unhappiness." (*CS*, 394 and 390) He reads them attentively. A new note creeps into the correspondence that signals his need to retreat: he asks her not to write every day. Then he changes his mind: he does want the daily letter, even if it's very brief, just two lines or one word, "but if I had to go without them I would suffer terribly." (*LM*, 100) Milena's health isn't good either; she has a hemorrhage. Other people's illnesses are Kafka's specialty; he peppers her with questions and worries about her money problems. The economic situation in Vienna is terrible. He believes that Milena goes hungry; it is a fact that she works for tips as a porter at the railroad station. He tries to send her money, but his awkwardness is such that he does not get her to accept his help. She continues to ask him to come to Vienna. Kafka refuses and justifies his refusal by his unwillingness to tell his director a lie; at the same time he doesn't want to tell him the truth—that he is going to see Milena.

Finally, at Kafka's suggestion, they agree to meet in Gmünd, halfway between Vienna and Prague. He writes "Please definitely come to Gmünd," but not before telling her that he had "feared" a night in Gmünd, but the "fear was only the usual 'fear' (which unfortunately is quite sufficient) I have in Prague as well; it wasn't any special fear of Gmünd." (*LM*, 148) Since in that letter he has given her an explanation of the role of fear and desire in his sexuality, which she could not have failed to understand, the prospect of the meeting must have been as troubling for her as for him. At the same time, thoughts of Milena's husband continue to preoccupy Kafka. In part, the reason is that now she seems unwilling to spend the night in Gmünd—an objection to the meeting he attributes to her feelings for

Polak and sweeps aside, pointing out that she can arrive by
a morning train and leave in the evening. On the day before
he is to go to Gmünd, he writes of her indissoluble marriage,
and comments bitterly on her worries about Polak:

> It's really very simple; if you were to leave him he'll
> either live with another woman or move into a board-
> ing house, and his boots will be polished better than
> they are now. This is silly and not silly, I don't know
> what it is about these remarks that causes me such
> pain. Maybe you know. (*LM*, 160)

The letters to Milena that precede the meeting in Gmünd
seem those of a man completely distraught and torn by the
conflict between love and anxieties and inhibitions. A letter
to Brod, written the day before the one to Milena about the
shopgirl and the dichotomy of fear and desire, shows the
other side of Kafka, the sane side that coexists with folly. In
it, he talks about progressing slowly in his reading of Brod's
new work on paganism, Christianity, and Judaism because
of "swimming weather in Prague," and goes on to offer
incisive comments on the chapters he has read. (*L*, 241)

The meeting in Gmünd is a failure—in the same class
as the botched encounters with Felice in the Tiergarten in
1913, and in Bodenbach two years later. The first explanation
of what has transpired between Kafka and Milena comes
in his letter of August 28. "I won't write about Gmünd
any more either," he tells her—"at least not intentionally,"
and continues:

> There'd be a lot to say, but in the end all it would
> come down to that the first day in Vienna wouldn't
> have been any better had I left in the evening. Even
> so, Vienna had the advantage over Gmünd because I
> arrived there half-unconscious with fear and exhaus-

tion, but when I arrived in Gmünd, on the other hand, I felt—although I didn't realize it, fool that I was—so grandly confident, as if nothing could happen to me any more. I went there like a homeowner.... (*LM*, 173)

It is difficult not to suppose that behind these circumlocutions lurks a failure: Kafka's desire having been overcome by fear, and his inability to forgive himself for it. Relations between them change, subtly at first but irremediably. She is unhappy; his doctor sees no improvement in his condition and recommends that he leave for a sanatorium. Two sanatoriums in Austria come under consideration. He tells her that in the end he may not go to either of them. He is afraid of sanatoriums for lung patients, "houses that literally cough and shake with fever day and night..." (*LM*, 177) An attempt he makes to get increased financial help for Milena from her father misfires. Faced with her reproaches, he tells her that "we have to stop writing to each other and leave the future to the future." (*LM*, 191) He thinks of himself as an animal lying in a dirty ditch that, forgetting what it is, has ventured close to her. She has been good to him; he has laid his face in her hand "so proud, so free, so mighty, so much at home," but he remains a mere animal. He refers to the tormenting discussions about "fear," and his growing conviction that for her he is "an unclean pest," so that, like a wild animal, he must withdraw into the dark. (*LM*, 194)

There is no end to his self-abasement. He sends her a drawing of a torture machine designed to draw and quarter the victim, and tells her that the inventor "is leaning against the column with his arms and legs crossed, putting on airs as if the whole thing were his invention, when all he really did was watch the butcher in front of his shop, drawing out a disemboweled pig." (*LM*, 201) In the same letter, he warns her that the person she is writing to doesn't exist, neither the one she met in Vienna nor the one in Gmünd, but if such a person did exist, it was really the one she had seen in Gmünd, "and may he be cursed." (*LM*, 201) The flow of the letters slows; they are shorter. Kafka returns to the subject of sanatoriums, settling for the time being on Grimmenstein in southern Austria. He points out that one can go easily from there to Wiener-Neustadt, itself accessible without difficulty from Vienna, and adds that "it probably doesn't make a great difference either to you or to me." He asks how it is possible that she is still not afraid of him or disgusted. (*LM*, 208)

Kafka's bitter and sometimes despairing reflections on Jewish identity and the hatred engulfing Jews accompany this strange *Liebestodt* duet, from which Milena's voice is unfortunately missing. He tells her about Russian-Jewish emigrants packed into the Rathaus, waiting for American visas. (*LM*, 190) As we have seen, he spends an afternoon in the streets during the November 1920 riots, "wallowing in anti-Semitic hate," realizing that the "heroism of staying on" is "merely the heroism of cockroaches that cannot be exterminated, even from the bathroom." (*LM*, 213) On the Graben, the choice place for an afternoon promenade, he writes, his Western-Jewish disguise falls off and he is left standing there naked with rags and scraps and pieces. (*LM*, 218) The threnody ends—or in any event moves into another register—with a letter written at the end of November 1920. "How can I believe you need my letters now," he writes,

when the only thing you need is peace, as you have so often said, half unconsciously. And these letters really are pure anguish, *they are caused by incurable anguish and they cause incurable anguish*. Moreover it's even getting worse—what good will my letters be this winter? The only way to live is to be silent and still, here as well as there. (*LM*, 222)

There will not be another letter until March 1922. When he writes her then he addresses her as Frau Milena, and uses the formal *Sie*. There is another handful of letters, the last one written on Christmas Day, 1923, that of a broken and dying man. But in 1920, after a lapse of almost two years, Kafka had resumed writing in his diary. On October 21, he recorded in it having given Milena all his diaries—except the new notebook he had just begun. (*D*, 392)

Apparently, Milena was not willing to accept the separation. Writing to Brod from Matliary in mid-April 1921, Kafka asks him to let him know when Milena comes to Prague, and how long she is staying, so that he won't return at that time, and to inform him if Milena should decide to go to the Tatras on account of her illness so that he might leave in plenty of time to avoid her. He acknowledges that his not wanting to see her is "an illness of instinct... She is unattainable for me," he continues,

> I must resign myself to that, and my energies are in such a state that they do so jubilantly. Which adds shame to my suffering; it is as if Napoleon had said to the demon that summoned him to Russia: "I cannot go now: I haven't drunk my evening glass of milk yet...." (*L*, 273)

At the beginning of May, writing to Brod from Matliary, he tells him:

> You are going to speak to M. I shall never again have this joy. When you speak to her about me, speak as you would of someone dead. When Ehrenstein [a mutual friend] saw me recently, he said in effect

that in M. life was reaching out to me and I had the choice between life and death. That was somewhat too magniloquent (not in regard to M. but in regard to me), but in essence it was true. It was only stupid that he seemed to believe that I had such a choice. If there were still a Delphic oracle, I would have asked it and it would have answered: "The choice between death and life? How can you hesitate?" (*L*, 279–80)

In fact, Milena visited Kafka four times in November 1921. He was again on medical leave, staying in his parents' apartment. On December 2, he noted:

Writing letters in my parents' room—the forms my decline takes are inconceivable! This thought lately, that as a little child I had been defeated by my father and because of ambition I have never been able to quit the battlefield all these years despite the perpetual defeats I suffer—always M. or not M.—but a principle, a light in the darkness! (*D*, 397)

Kafka suffered a complete nervous collapse in January 1922. The diary entry for January 16 gives an indication of its severity:

This past week I suffered something very like a breakdown; the only one to match it was on that night two years ago; apart from then I have never experienced its like. Everything seemed over with, even today, there is no great improvement to be noticed.... Impossible to sleep, impossible to stay awake, impossible to endure life, or, more exactly, the course of life. The clocks are not in unison; the inner one runs crazily on a devilish or demoniac or in any case inhuman pace, the other one limps along at its usual speed. What else can happen but that the two worlds split apart, and when they do split apart, or at least clash in a fearful manner. (*D*, 398–9)

It is difficult not to attribute the breakdown to grief. On December 1, 1921, Kafka wrote in his diary: "I feel no sorrow at her departure, no real sorrow, it is a long way from this unconcern to the point where her departure would cause me endless sorrow." (*D*, 397) But diary entries for the following January show that thoughts of Milena and lost opportunities for fulfillment continued to torment him. Still in Prague, he wrote on January 18:

> What have you done with your gift of sex? It was a failure, in the end that is all they will say. But it might easily have succeeded.
>
> Sex keeps gnawing at me, hounds me day and night, I should have to conquer fear and shame and probably sorrow too to satisfy it; yet on the other hand I am certain that I should take advantage with no feeling of fear or sorrow or shame, of the first opportunity to present itself quickly, close at hand, and willingly....(*D*, 400)

The next day's entry sets out two questions that he would have liked to address to her:

> Because of several piddling signs I am ashamed to mention, it was my impression that your recent visits were indeed kind and noble as ever but somewhat tiresome to you nevertheless, somewhat forced, too, like the visits one pays an invalid. Is my impression correct? Did you find in the diaries some final proof against me? (*D*, 401)

Seeking a remedy, Kafka's physician personally took him to Spindlermühle, a mountain resort in Bohemian Riesengebirge, a mountain chain between the upper courses of the Elbe and the Oder. On January 29, two days after his arrival, Kafka wrote:

> If M., for example, should suddenly come here, it would be dreadful. Externally, indeed, my situation would at once seem comparatively brighter. I should be esteemed as one human being among others. I should have words spoken to me that were more than merely polite. I should sit at the actors' table (less erect, it is true, when I am sitting here alone, though even now I am slumped down); outwardly I should be almost a match in conviviality for Dr. H. [his physician]—yet I should be plunged into a world in which I could not live. It only remains to solve the riddle of why I had fourteen days of happiness [with Felice], and why, consequently, I might perhaps also be able to be happy here with M. (though of course only after a painful breakdown of barriers). But the difficulties would probably be much greater than in Marienbad, my opinions are more rigid, my experience larger. What used to be a dividing thread is now a wall, or a mountain range, or rather a grave. (*D*, 409)

Two months later he mentioned wanting to write to her. (*D*, 418) No corresponding letter exists. They saw each other again, perhaps on April 26 (*D*, 419), and certainly on May 8 or some days earlier. (*D*, 420) But the wished-for and dreaded end of his great love affair had come, and there could be no hope of a new beginning.

LEFT: Herman Kafka, Franz's father

RIGHT: Julie Löwy, Franz's mother

LEFT: Kafka at about two
RIGHT: About five

LEFT: Undated picture of Kafka's three sisters.
Left to right: Valli, Elli, Ottla

RIGHT: Max Brod

Milena Jesenská

LEFT: Grete Bloch
RIGHT: Dora Diamant

Kafka with Felice Bauer, in 1917

Kafka in 1917, at thirty-one

Kafka's 1915 passport photo

LEFT: A photo taken in 1908 for Kafka's employee pass at the Insurance Institute

RIGHT: Ottla at eighteen

1906 photo of Kafka with the waitress Hansi Julie Szokoll

Kafka in a photo taken
by Max Brod during
their university days

The last photo, circa 1923

IV

I am made of literature, I am nothing else.

Kafka's life commands so imperatively our interest because his short stories and novels stand among the most original and greatest works of twentieth-century literature. Without them, there would be little to remember him for: this very private and withdrawn man would have been just another German-speaking Jew among 146,098 Christians and Jews, Czech- and German-speaking, who died in Czechoslovakia in 1924, the same year as he. As we have seen, Kafka's work for the Insurance Institute, however valuable and appreciated by his superiors, was, so far as he was concerned, nothing but a meaningless void that sucked away the time and energy needed for his real life's work, which was writing. Apart from moments of triumph, when a work he had completed met his superbly exigent standards, the only significant events in his private and humdrum life were occasional infatuations and the ups and downs of his relations with Felice and Milena, which we have followed, and, of course, the milestones marking the progress of his illness.

To trace the latter, we must go back in time. In September 1917, after the hemorrhage, the Institute granted Kafka a three-month sick leave. As we have seen, he joined Ottla in Zürau. Due to her efforts, the leave was extended, permitting him to remain with her for most of another three months. The experience was of capital importance not only because of the tranquil happiness he drew from Ottla's presence but also because the primitive rural life he was able to observe served later as raw material for *The Castle*. He returned to work at the Institute in May 1918. Six months later, he came down with Spanish influenza, a victim of the pandemic that claimed fifty to one hundred million lives worldwide. His lungs already seriously weakened by tuberculosis, he developed double pneumonia and recovered with difficulty. On November 30, his mother took him by train to Schelesen, a village in northern Bohemia, for a rest-and-fresh-air cure recommended by the family doctor. He stayed at the Pension Stüdl, where he met the beguiling Julie Wohryzek.

He was back in Prague in March 1919, his health not much improved. It continued to worsen during the rest of that year and on into 1920. At the beginning of April 1920, he traveled to Merano, well known as a center for the treatment of lung patients, and checked into the Pension Ottoburg. The letters to Milena preceding their four-day tryst in Vienna were all written from there. His health deteriorated further during the fall and winter of 1920–21. Acting this time on her own initiative, Ottla obtained for him yet another sick leave, which enabled him to depart at the end of December 1920 for a sanatorium in Matliary. Eight months there accomplished little; at best the disease may have been temporarily held in check. After six months he wrote Brod that getting better was "out of the question." Even his doctor thought that a cure was improbable. (*L*, 280) Nevertheless, upon his return to Prague at the end of August, he resumed work at the Institute. It was not a wise decision. A mere two months later, he was again placed on medical leave, this one obtained by his alarmed parents, and ultimately extended until April 1922. The plan was to attempt a cure consisting of bed rest, moderate exercise, and other palliative measures. The results were mixed. In January 1922, as previously described, there was a grave new complication: Kafka's nervous breakdown. The stay

in Spindlermühle recommended by his physician did not
succeed in causing the tuberculosis to retreat, but Kafka
sledded, hiked, and even thought of skiing.

Above all, he was once again writing. "First Sorrow"
and "A Hunger Artist" were written in Spindlermühle; in
all probability, Kafka began writing *The Castle* there as well.
Breaking the pattern of having to be coaxed by Brod into
publishing, Kafka spontaneously submitted the stories to
two periodicals, *Genius* and *Neue Rundschau*. He returned
to Prague in March, and, at the beginning of April, told his
friend Robert Klopstock that:

> after being lashed through periods of insanity, I began
> to write, and this writing is the most important thing
> in the world to me (in a way that is horrible to everyone
> around me, so unspeakably horrible that I don't talk
> about it)—the way his delusion is important to the
> madman (should he lose it, he would become "mad")
> or the way her pregnancy is important to a woman.
> This has nothing to do with the value of the writing—I
> know that value only too precisely, just as I know the
> value it has for me.... And so with trembling fear
> I protect the writing from every disturbance, and
> not writing alone, but the solitude that is part of it.
> (*L*, 323)

In April, Kafka obtained another extension of his sick leave
and added to it the weeks that would have represented his
normal vacation. Working on *The Castle*, he wanted to
wall himself off from disturbances. "The amount of quiet
I need," he wrote, "is not to be found on the face of this
earth. For at least a year I would like to hide myself away
with my notebook and talk to no one. The merest nothing
shatters me." (*L*, 325)

Unfortunately, it had become clear once more that there was no improvement in his physical condition, and the Institute's own physician found him unfit for service. There was no choice: at the age of 39, Kafka applied for retirement. The application was granted as of July 1, 1922. His pension was fixed at about one-third of the salary he would have received as senior secretary of the Institute, the post to which he had been recently promoted, an amount that could just about cover his very modest needs. However, as we know, in September 1923, he would move to Berlin, and there the value of his pension melted away in German hyperinflation.

For the first time since he went to work for the Institute he was free do as he liked. Toward the end of June, he joined Ottla and her one-year-old daughter Vera in Planá, a small town about fifty miles south from Prague, where she and her family had taken an apartment for the summer. He remained there, with short interruptions, for nearly three months, working on *The Castle* and a short story, "The Investigations of a Dog." Toward the end of August, he abandoned work on the novel. He found himself likewise unable to complete the short story. Looking back, he wrote in his diary on September 26: "With some exceptions, a good period thanks to Ottla." (*D*, 422) The exceptions were an anxiety attack that prevented him from joining Oskar Baum and his wife in Georgental, a village in the Thuringian Forest; the suffering caused him by the noise of children playing in the street; a trip to Prague to see his father that he thought was a failure; and yet another anxiety attack brought on by the fear that Ottla's departure for Prague would oblige him to remain alone in Planá during September.

An even drearier period opened upon his return to Prague. As before, he lived at his family's apartment.

Writing to Minze Eisner, an orphaned young woman he had befriended in Schelesen, he tried to make light of his illness:

> It is not as bad as it looks from outside the closed door of the sickroom, but the building is a bit fragile. However, I am better by now and two months ago was in fine shape. It is merely a somewhat confused war situation. The disease itself viewed as combat troops is the most obedient creature in the world: it keeps its eyes fixed entirely on headquarters and carries out whatever orders are issued there. Up there, though, they are often indecisive and there are other causes of misunderstanding. Something should be done to end the split between headquarters and troops. (*L*, 364)

Nothing could be done; his health was failing rapidly. Visits from friends tired him. He went out less and less and wrote fewer letters. The next-to-last entry in his diary for 1922, dated November 14, reads: "Always 99.6 degrees, 99.9 in the evening. Sit at the desk, get nothing done, am hardly ever in the street…" (*D*, 423) Toward the end of the year, an infection caused him to suffer severe cramps in the stomach and bowel, as well as a high fever. He took to his bed. To these miseries was added the return of total insomnia, which he thought would drive him to the verge of insanity, and with it the need for sleeping pills.

Kafka's interest in everything Jewish had been growing since the end of the war. The rise of the nationalist Czechoslovak state had put in question the position of the German-speaking minority as a whole: it was no longer ascendant politically or culturally and its new role was unclear. At the Institute, power passed practically overnight out of the hands of German-speaking officials, and Kafka was finding it expedient to write in Czech to the new Czech director of the Institute concerning his medical situation and requests for leave. The situation of German-speaking Jews was uniquely uncomfortable. They were caught in a vise. Not only were they in the wrong political, cultural, and linguistic camp; they also had to face both Czech and German anti-Semitism, the Czech variety having manifested itself in 1919 and 1920 by mob violence that continued sporadically until Masaryk, having become president of the Republic, was able to calm the country. Kafka's severe illness and depression exacerbated his sense of personal vulnerability as well as alienation from German culture, the only community to which, as a great master of German prose, he truly belonged. His response included a renewed effort to learn Hebrew.

In early 1923, he began to take lessons at the family apartment from Puah Ben-Tovim, a nineteen-year-old girl born in Palestine. Puah was in Prague at the instigation of Hugo Bergmann, Kafka's school and university friend, staying with his parents and studying mathematics at the university. By coincidence, Bergmann, who had emigrated to Palestine, had come to Prague as well, on a short visit. He tried to persuade Kafka to fulfill his old wish and move to Palestine, offering the hospitality of his apartment in Jerusalem. Kafka said he was tempted, but the project was postponed until at least the fall, the stated and obvious reason being that he had to find out first whether he would be able to travel. For the time being, he had agreed to go in July to Müritz, a German resort on the Baltic, and stay there with his sister Elli and her family. He wrote to Bergmann: "To test my transportability, after many years of lying abed and of headaches, I pulled myself together for a short trip to the Baltic Sea." (*L*, 372) That was on July 13; in a letter to Frau Bergmann written later that month he made clear that he was unable to go to Palestine: "Once again the temptation beckons, and again the absolute impossibility answers." (*L*, 374)

In Müritz, Kafka discovered that near his hotel was a summer camp for Jewish refugee children from Eastern Europe. He met there Dora Diamant, a twenty-five-year-old woman from Poland, raised in a Hasidic family, who was working in the kitchen. The attraction between them was immediate, but on August 9 Kafka felt obliged to return to Prague. He was sicker than ever. Ottla did not wish him to stay in the city and induced him to come to Schelesen with her and her children. His health didn't improve there. On August 29, he wrote to Brod from Schelesen: "There isn't much to say about it; I'm trying to gain a little weight— when I came here I weighed 54 ½ kilos [125 lbs], have never weighed so little—but I can scarcely manage it. Too many counter forces." (*L*, 379)

Sickness and depression notwithstanding, Kafka's rigor when it came to judging his own work had not diminished. In September, an opportunity came to earn 1,000 Swiss francs—a large sum for that time—in the form of an invitation from a Swiss publisher to submit a work for publication. Kafka refused, telling the publisher that "[t]he writings I have on hand from an earlier period are altogether useless; I cannot show them to anybody." (*L*, 380) The work that Kafka so unequivocally found wanting would, of course, eventually be published through Brod's efforts.

During the stay in Schelesen, also in September, Kafka made plans to move to Berlin and live there with Dora. He returned to Prague for two days, September 22 and 23, to collect clothes and other possessions, and, at the age of forty, to face his parents' recriminations over this show of independence. On September 25 he was at last in Berlin with Dora. Writing to Oskar Baum to apologize for not having gone to see him when he passed through Prague, he gave the impression that his stay in Berlin wouldn't be long:

> How could I have come, faced with the foolhardy prospect of going to Berlin for a few days. Within the limits of my condition that is a foolhardiness whose parallel you can only find by leafing back through the pages of history, say to Napoleon's march to Russia. Outwardly, and for the present it is going tolerably well, as it did back then, by the way. (*L*, 382)

Perhaps he wasn't sure of his plans. In fact Kafka remained in Berlin, where he had so often dreamed of settling, for six months.

Notwithstanding his rapidly worsening condition, Kafka's correspondence throughout the Berlin period was remarkably lucid and often irrepressibly gay. He reported on the efforts he made to keep an eye on Brod's mistress, Emmy Salveter, by then a popular actress, and mediated between her and Brod, offering wise and sensitive advice to both parties. He worried about Klopstock and inquired avidly about his friends' books. Brod had been working on his novel *Reubeni*: Kafka wanted to know whether he had finished it. (*L*, 390) In a later letter, written when he was already running a high fever, having heard that Brod had resumed work on the novel, he sent him best wishes. He read reviews by Brod published in *Abendblatt*, including the review of a play by Werfel then being performed in Prague, and commented on them (*L*, 399); he asked whether Brod's new play *Bunterbart* had been performed, explaining that because of the inflation he no longer bought newspapers; told Brod of Dora's delighted response to an essay of his that she had read. (*L*, 401) In January, although suffering from a high fever, he discussed the implications of the negative reviews of Brod's play (*L*, 404) and apologized for not having written to Oskar Baum about a story Baum had published in the German periodical *Rundschau*. Kafka was a pitiless and astute critic of literature. There can be no doubt that he knew that his own work—however flawed he found most of it to be—stood on a level immeasurably higher than Brod's, Werfel's, or Baum's, but there is no longer a trace of envy of their successes to be found in the letters, or self-pity when he compared, as he must have, their relatively normal lives and steady literary output with the parched desert of his own existence. He had been purged of every trace of base feeling.

Scattered throughout the Berlin correspondence are references to his efforts to continue learning Hebrew and immerse himself in Jewish matters. They were the lifeline he was clutching. Thus he discusses with Emmy Salveter their perhaps attending Sukkot (the Jewish harvest festival). (*L*, 383) He worries about not receiving *Selbstwehr*, the Jewish periodical to which he subscribed and read avidly; he questions his sister Valli about the Jewish school in Prague and the progress made by his niece Lotte in Hebrew. (*L*, 396–7) He tells Felix Weltsch, the editor of *Selbstwehr*, that when the weather is good he attends sessions at the Academy for Jewish Studies twice a week; and he reports to Brod repeatedly in deprecating terms about his attempts to continue learning Hebrew. (*L*, 388, 389) He writes to Ottla about Klopstock, who was studying medicine in Prague: "If only one could help him a little, at least in practical matters; he has no room, his free meal privilege is threatened, he's injured his hand, he's facing a difficult examination, he probably has no money either…" (*LO*, 80)

Whether Klopstock is keeping up his connection with Jews is a particular worry. Already in a letter from Müritz Kafka had asked: "Would you feel like moving to Berlin? Closer, very close to the Jews?" (*L*, 378) In a letter from Berlin, he prods him: doesn't the study of chemistry "also

leave some room for Hebrew?" (*L*, 390) He advises him
to stop doing translations and think of doing his own
work; he should return to his native town in Hungary,
"fleeing into silence" after the doctoral examinations, even
though "an overwhelming abundance of Hebrew affairs
is being planned in Prague." (*L*, 392) As for himself, he
tells Klopstock that

> You must not imagine...that my life is such that I
> have the freedom to report, or even to write, at any
> given moment. There are abysses into which I sink
> without even noticing, only at best to creep up again
> after a long time. Such are not the proper occasions
> for writing. (*L*, 402)

The abysses were his illness and dire penury. The
hyperinflation in Germany—food prices rose by 13,573%
from July 1922 to July 1923—had been checked abruptly
in November 1923 through measures taken by Hjalmar
Schacht, the president of the Reichsbank, which came to be
known as the Schacht Miracle. But although hyperinflation
was over, prices continued to rise. Kafka's pension was paid
by the Institute in Czech crowns, a relatively strong currency,
and Kafka's parents sent it in cash by mail or through friends
traveling to Berlin in order to avoid unnecessary bank-
transfer and conversion charges. But for people like Kafka
and Dora, living on a fixed monthly remittance, making
ends meet remained difficult if not impossible. Adding to
the sense of doom was the political situation in Germany.
Thus, On October 25, he wrote to Brod that

> from the front pages of the newspapers on display [at
> the publishers' branches in his neighborhood] I absorb
> the poison that I can just manage to bear, sometimes
> momentarily cannot bear (just now there is talk in the

anteroom about street battles). But then I leave this
public place and lose myself, if I still have the strength,
in the quiet autumnal avenues. (*L*, 388)

He was referring to the pandemic of strikes and violence
fomented by political extremists of the right and the left.

Meanwhile, the ravages of tuberculosis had accelerated.
In mid-January 1924, he explained to Brod that he had
not written earlier because he had been sick with fever
and chills. The doctor called to his bedside asked for 160
crowns that Dora negotiated down to half that. "Since
then," he continued,

I have had a tenfold fear of getting sick; a second-class
bed in the Jewish Hospital costs 64 crowns a day, but
that only pays for bed and board, apparently not for
service of a doctor...(*L*, 403)

In late February or early March, Uncle Siegfried, the Triesch
doctor, traveled to Berlin to check on Kafka's condition.
Following the visit, Kafka wrote to Klopstock that

we'll soon be coming to Prague; if a sanatorium in
the Vienna woods proves feasible, then certainly. I
am resisting a sanatorium, also resisting staying at
a pension, but what's the use since I cannot resist
the fever. And 100.4 has become my daily bread, all
evening long and half the night...on account of the
fever I have not been out of the house for weeks, feel
strong enough while lying down, but if I attempt
any walks, after the first step they assume the quality of a grandiose enterprise so that sometimes the
thought of peacefully burying myself alive in the
sanatorium is not all so unpleasant....But then comes
that morning and evening coughing lasting for hours,

and the flask almost full every day—that again argues
for the sanatorium. But then again there is fear, for
example of the horrible compulsory eating there.
(*L*, 409–10)

In reality, his uncle had advised Kafka to travel directly to a
sanatorium in Vienna or Davos; it was Kafka who insisted
on going first to Prague. Max Brod, who happened to
have come to Berlin to attend the première of Janácek's
opera *Jenufa*, which he had translated into German from
the Czech, brought Kafka back to Prague, to his parents'
apartment.

He stayed there for three weeks, cared for first by
Klopstock and, after her arrival in Prague at the end of
March, also by Dora. She had remained in Berlin at Kafka's
insistence. During the Berlin period, Kafka had written
to Dora's Hasid father asking for her hand. Her father
consulted the rebbe of Gere, the Hasid *shtetl* in Eastern
Poland where the father lived. The rebbe's one-word
verdict was: No. Kafka didn't want now to expose her to
remarks his parents might make about her living with him
out of wedlock. On April 7, Dora took Kafka to the Wiener
Wald Sanatorium, located in the near vicinity of Vienna. He
weighed less than one hundred pounds. There he learned
that he had tuberculosis of the larynx. Having watched the
torment of his fellow patient at the Matliary who had been
afflicted by that form of the disease, he understood what
lay in store for him. After a visit to the bedside of the sick
man, he had written to Brod:

What you see in that bed is much worse than an execution, yes, even than a torturing. To be sure, we have not
ourselves invented the tortures but have learned about
them from diseases, and no man dares to torture the
way they do. Here torture goes on for years, with pauses

for effect so that it will not go too quickly, and—the unique element—the victim himself is compelled by his own will, out of his wretched inner self, to protract the torture. This whole wretched life in bed, the fever, the shortness of breath, the taking of medicines… all this has no other purpose but to slow down the development of the abscesses, from which he must eventually suffocate, to prolong this wretched life, the fever, and so on, as long as possible. (*L*, 253)

The Matliary patient, as Kafka had learned soon afterward, had thrown himself under a train. Kafka endured the torture; fortunately it was of short duration.

From Wiener Wald he was transferred to a university clinic in Vienna itself, and from there he was taken on April 19, over the objections of the attending physician, to the much smaller and more pleasant sanatorium in Kierling, a town northeast of Vienna. Klopstock joined Dora there and helped her care for him. On May 11, Brod visited Kafka for the last time, and on May 19 (the date is not certain), Kafka wrote to his parents. He discouraged them from coming to visit. "I am still not very pretty," he told them,

not at all a sight worth seeing.… If you also count in the fact that I am allowed to speak only in whispers and even that not too often, you will gladly postpone the visit.… Since I cannot show the visitors—and what is more, such visitors as you two would be—major, undeniable progress, measurable even by the eyes, I think we should rather let it be. (*L*, 414–5)

In the preceding weeks, the need for money for medical expenses had turned out to be a powerful spur. Kafka mustered enough strength to write during those terrible days "Josephine, the Singer, or the Mouse Folk," a tale of a diva who sings in a whisper, and on April 9, when he was already in the Sanatorium Wiener Wald, wrote to Brod about publishing the story:

> It [the sanatorium] is expensive, might very well be frightfully expensive; "Josephine" must help a little, there is no other way. Please offer it to Otto Pick [a friend who was a journalist] (of course he can print what he likes from Meditation); if he takes it, please send it to Die Schmiede [a German publisher] later; if he doesn't take it, then send it right away. As for me, it's evidently the larynx. (*L*, 411–2)

Brod did give the story to Pick, who used his influence with the editor-in-chief of *Präger Presse*, a German-language newspaper published in Prague, with the result that "Josephine" was published in the literary supplement of the paper's Easter issue, on April 20, 1924. As for Die Schmiede, Kafka had already submitted there three of his latest stories, "A Hunger Artist," "First Sorrow," and "A Little Woman." On his deathbed, Kafka corrected the proof of the first sixteen pages of *A Hunger Artist*, a volume that consisted of those stories and "Josephine."

Soon after he had entered the Kierling sanatorium, Kafka was no longer able even to whisper. To make himself understood, he had to write notes to Dora and Klopstock and to the examining doctor. They have been preserved, and they are heartbreaking. For instance:

> A little water; these bits of pills stick in the mucus like splinters of glass.

> To think that once I could simply venture a large swallow of water.

Can the pain temporarily stop? I mean, for a fairly long time?

How many years will you be able to stand it? How long will I be able to stand your standing it?

Put your hand on my forehead for a moment to give me courage. (*L*, 416–21)

One's feelings for Kafka easily become fraternal, so that his missteps, defeats, and sorrows affect one deeply, as though they were one's own. After so much torment, this marvelous man died at noon, on June 3, 1924, a month before his forty-first birthday. His body was taken to Prague, where he was buried on June 11, in the Strašnice Jewish Cemetery. His parents were later buried alongside him. A single stone marks the three graves.

No one understood Kafka better than Milena. He bared himself to her completely. The eulogy she wrote for *Národní Listy*, a Prague daily, was published on June 6 and has never been equaled:

Few people knew him here, for he was a recluse, a wise man in dread of life.... He once wrote in a letter: when heart and soul can't bear it any longer, the lung takes on half the burden, so that it is distributed a little more evenly—and that's the way it was with his disease. It lent him an almost miraculous tenderness and an almost horribly uncompromising intellectual refinement.... He was shy, anxious, meek, and kind, yet the books he wrote are gruesome and painful. He saw the world as full of invisible demons, tearing apart and destroying defenseless humans. He was too clairvoyant, too intelligent to be capable of living, and too weak to fight. He was weak the way noble, beautiful people are, people incapable of struggling against their fear of misunderstanding, malice, or intellectual deceit because they recognize their own helplessness in advance; their submission only shames the victor. He understood people as only someone of great and nervous sensitivity can, someone who is alone, someone who can recognize others in a flash, almost like a prophet. His knowledge of the world was extraordinary and deep; he was himself an extraordinary and deep world.... He was an artist and man of such anxious conscience he could hear even where others, deaf, felt themselves secure. (*LM*, 271–2)

V

The axe for the frozen sea inside us...

In a letter dated January 27, 1904, Kafka wrote to his friend Oskar Pollak,

> If the book we're reading doesn't wake us up with a blow on the head, what are we reading it for?…We need books to affect us like a disaster, that grieve us deeply, like the death of someone we loved more than ourselves, like being banished into forests far from everyone, like a suicide. A book must be the axe for the frozen sea inside us. (*L*, 16)

Kafka met that lofty standard eight years later, at the age of twenty-nine, when he wrote "The Judgment." (*CS*, 77) Nothing he had written before had come close. It has been suggested that he had destroyed juvenilia composed before 1904 in response to Pollak's harsh criticism, so that the earliest surviving works anterior to "The Judgment" are *Description of a Struggle* (*CS*, 9), *Wedding Preparations in the Country* (*CS*, 52), on which Kafka had worked intermittently between 1904 and 1908, after his friendship with Pollak had cooled, and eight short prose pieces written between 1904 and 1908 that appeared in *Hyperion*. Much of this work is overwritten and fey, probably due to the influence of a style prevalent in *Der Kunstwart*, a periodical devoted to the arts, to which Pollak had introduced Kafka. (*B*, 54, 57) It is not surprising that Kafka wanted the work destroyed. With the single exception of "Bachelor's Ill Luck" (*CS*, 394), my dislike extends, for the same reasons, to *Meditation*, a collection of eighteen prose pieces published by Rowohlt in 1913. Kafka must have shared my view of this slender volume for, as we have seen, in his first letter of instructions to Brod concerning his personal papers, he wrote:

> The few copies of *Meditation* can remain. I do not want to give anyone the trouble of pulping them; but nothing in that volume must be printed again. (*T*, 266)

Certainly there are striking sentences and insights to be found in the work that preceded "The Judgment," and it was doubtless possible to believe—as Max Brod claimed he did when he heard Kafka read aloud from *Wedding Preparations*—that they heralded the appearance of a literary genius. (*B*, 60–1) A genius, perhaps, but not yet a great writer.

The great writer revealed himself in "The Judgment," composed in a burst of creativity during the night of September 22–23, 1912, one day after Yom Kippur, the Jewish Day of Atonement. Seemingly overnight, Kafka had mastered the art of storytelling. He would never again write a story that failed to hold the reader captive until the last word on the last page. "The Judgment" also unveiled one of Kafka's great inventions—perhaps the greatest: the nonchalant treatment of events in his fiction that every reader knows are implausible (in "The Judgment," *In the Penal Colony*, and *The Trial*), or outright impossible (in *The Metamorphosis* or "A Report to an Academy"). Kafka wrote of them as though they were unquestionably happening or had happened, their presumed truth being buttressed by painstakingly detailed descriptions. As we read, we accept their reality, just as before awakening we accept our dreams as real. One consequence, quintessential to Kafka's art, is that in his created world there is no room for surprise. The Samsa family in *The Metamorphosis* is horrified and shocked to see that Gregor has turned a giant beetle, but neither his parents nor his sister evince anything like astonishment; in *In the Penal Colony* the explorer finds the judicial system repugnant, but doesn't ask himself whether he is in the midst of a nightmare; in *The Trial*, Joseph K.'s truculence keeps pace with his growing understanding of the bizarre workings of the court processes, but he doesn't challenge their reality. Instead, he tells the Inspector that he is "by no means very much surprised" by the strangeness of the circumstances of his arrest. In Kafka's world, the story is what it is: reality is as portrayed. We are riveted by monologues delivered by a dog, an ape, or a canny animal warily patrolling the corridors of its burrow. Another aspect of Kafka's placid narration is that it encourages, sometimes irresistibly, interpretation of the work. Since we all know that, for instance, people don't turn into insects, and apes don't address academies, we ask ourselves: what did Kafka really mean to tell us? Digging hard to find a meaning that one thinks hidden in a work of fiction is beneficial when it leads to the reader's treating its text with all the respect it deserves. Mischief comes when theories and interpretations upstage the text, deflect attention from its beauty, or narrow its import.

The September 1912 night of wonder inaugurated a period of sustained creativity that proved unmatched. It coincided with Kafka's courtship of Felice, and lasted until shortly after the hemorrhage of August 1917. In addition to "The Judgment," before the end of 1912 Kafka wrote *The Metamorphosis* (*CS*, 89) and "The Stoker" (published as a separate story in 1913, it was the opening chapter of *Amerika*). He wrote *In the Penal Colony* (*CS*, 140) in the fall of 1914. Most of *The Trial* and the last chapter of *Amerika* he was able to get down on paper during that fall, but work on *The Trial* spilled over into January 1915. Not much else was accomplished in 1915, but in the fall of 1916, Kafka began to write at the little house on Alchimistengasse. It was there that Kafka wrote the stories that were eventually included in *A Country Doctor*. In addition to the title story and "A Report to an Academy," both of which stand at the highest level of Kafka's creation, the volume contained other works of high quality: "An Imperial Message," "The Cares of a Family Man," and "Fratricide."

Kafka was not productive in 1918, 1919, or 1920, if one discounts the two groups of aphorisms composed between October 1917 and January 1920, and the astounding *Letter to His Father* written in Schelesen in November 1919. Notwithstanding its personal importance to him, he manifestly did not think of the *Letter* as part of his literary oeuvre. April 1920 opens the Milena period. It ended effectively in November of that year. Whether because of emotional turmoil caused by that relationship or physical weakness, Kafka was unable to write in 1920 or 1921. The last spurt of masterful production began paradoxically with the breakdown of January 1922. In February of that year, he wrote "A Hunger Artist"; in January or in February he started *The Castle*, on which he worked through the end of August. In July he retired from the Institute and wrote the mysterious and heart-wrenching "Investigations of a Dog." None of the stories Kafka wrote in or after 1922 surpassed the best of the published production of 1912–17, but "Investigations of a Dog" and "The Burrow," written in October–December 1923 (*CS*, 325), both of which were published posthumously, as well as "A Hunger Artist" and "Josephine the Singer, or the Mouse Folk," written in March 1924 and published in Kafka's lifetime, are all at the same high level.

In 1916, Kafka told his publisher, Kurt Wolff, that "The Judgment" was his favorite story. (*L*, 126) He thought that it and two other short works he had completed were linked, and expressed the wish—not fulfilled in Kafka's lifetime—that they be issued in one volume:

> "The Stoker," The Metamorphosis...and "The Judgment" belong together, both inwardly and outwardly. There is an obvious connection among the three and, even more important, a secret one, for which reason I would be reluctant to forgo the chance to have them published together in a book, which might be called The Sons....You see, I am just as much concerned about the unity of the three stories as I am about the unity of any one of them. (*L*, 96–7)

The "obvious connection" is that in each of these works a father triumphs over his son. Kafka did not divulge the "secret" connection, but it may be deduced from a 1915 letter to his publisher. Having written *In the Penal Colony* the preceding year, Kafka presented him with a new idea: to publish *In the Penal Colony*, together with the three earlier stories, under the collective title of *Punishments*. (*L*, 113) The connection that thus emerges among the four stories is the treatment in each of them of guilt and retribution, a theme that also links them to *The Trial*. A separate thematic link is the urban setting, strongly suggestive of Kafka's Prague, of "The Judgment," *The Metamorphosis*, and *The Trial*, and the sour lower-middle-class milieu in which their action is played out.

In the Penal Colony made Kafka uneasy. Two years after finishing it, he wrote to Kurt Wolff:

> Your criticism of the painful element [in *Penal Colony*] accords completely with my opinion, but then I feel

the same way about almost everything I have written so far. Have you noticed how few things are free of this painful element in one form or another? By way of clarifying this last story, I need only add that the painfulness is not peculiar to it alone but our times in general and my own time as well have been painful and continue to be, and my own more consistently than the times.

He added: "I suppose it is also inappropriate for a public reading, although I am scheduled to read it in the Goltz Bookshop in November and I mean to do so. (*L*, 127) (As mentioned previously, the reading in Munich was not well received.)

A year later, after responding to Wolff's proposal to publish *A Country Doctor*, he returned to the subject of *Penal Colony*:

Perhaps there is some misunderstanding concerning "Penal Colony." I have never been entirely whole-hearted in asking for it to be published. Two or three of the final pages are botched, and their presence points to some deeper flaw; there is a worm somewhere which hollows out the story, dense as it is. Your offer to publish this story in the same manner as the *Country Doctor* is of course very tempting and excites me so much that I am ready to drop my defenses—nevertheless please do not publish the story, at least for the present. If you stood in my place and saw the story from my viewpoint, you would not think I was being overscrupulous in this matter. (*L*, 136)

Kafka's unease and continued preoccupation with the story continued, as shown by diary entries in 1917 that suggest variants. (*D*, 376, 380, 381–2) In a letter in January of the same year, to Gottfried Kölwel, a German poet, referred to *In the Penal Colony* as "my filthy story." (*L*, 129) But he didn't modify the story, and in 1919 Wolff finally published the text as initially submitted.

Gustav Janouch recalled in his memoir Kafka's remark that "[t]he Marquis de Sade, whose biography you lent to me, is the real patron of our era." (*J*, 131) The meaning of this pronouncement is obscure, but manifestly Kafka was aware of de Sade's work—or at last his reputation—and with *Penal Colony* Kafka crossed a thin but recognizable line, and entered the domain of the Marquis. This was a misstep he avoided when he wrote "A Report to an Academy" and "A Hunger Artist," two exceptionally cruel stories.

In *In the Penal Colony* an explorer visiting a tropical island is invited to witness an execution. His guide is an officer, who is also sole judge and executioner. He tells the explorer his "guiding principle: Guilt is never to be doubted." (*CS*, 145) The crime of the soldier condemned to die is that he did not submit passively to the horsewhipping administered by an officer whose room he was guarding. The punishment—torture until death, which usually comes within twelve hours—will be inflicted by the Harrow, an ingenious machine that inscribes the commandment the doomed man has breached on his torso. In this case, it is "Honor Thy Superiors." The Harrow writes with needles that first penetrate the skin and in later stages the flesh. The officer dwells on every detail of the operation: first the condemned man's hands and feet are strapped to the bed under the Harrow. A felt gag is stuffed into his mouth, and later removed once he has stopped screaming. At that point, he is given to lap with his tongue rice gruel in an electrically heated dish. His strength must be kept up, the officer explains, for the last six hours of the ordeal; after the sixth hour, an expression of enlightenment, highly appreciated by aficionados of the torture, spreads over the face of the condemned man, because he begins to read with his body, and understand, the commandment the Harrow has inscribed in his flesh.

The officer has a confession to make: the Harrow is not functioning perfectly. It needs replacement parts but they cannot be obtained, because the current commandant of the colony is determined to subvert the penal system, which was the invention of the Old Commandant. Worse yet, the officer suspects that that the new commandant intends to use the explorer's anticipated disapproval of torture as an argument for putting an end to its practice. But if the explorer, after having watched the Harrow at work, is in fact favorably impressed, perhaps he will become one of the Harrow's supporters and express that support to the new commandant, preferably in public.

The explorer has been thinking. Even granted that this is a penal colony, where extraordinary measures are needed to enforce discipline, he hasn't been satisfied by the explanation of the judicial procedure. At the same time, even though he has been highly recommended to the local authorities, it is always a ticklish proposition to meddle in other people's affairs: he risks being told to keep out. Therefore he gives a neutral answer: "he can neither help nor hinder." (*CS*, 157) The officer's renewed plea for support is violent and desperate, but the explorer, "fundamentally honorable and unafraid," stands firm. "I do not approve of your procedures," he tells the officer. And then he adds, "I shall tell the commandant what I think of the procedure, certainly, but not at a public conference, only in private." (*CS*, 160)

The officer has stopped listening. He smiles like "an old man [smiles] at childish nonsense and yet pursues his own meditations behind the smile," and orders the condemned man set free. (*CS*, 160) Then, having taken off his uniform with loving care and broken his sword, he lies down on the bed of the Harrow. The machinery spontaneously begins its work and starts to inscribe on his body a different and not inappropriate commandment: "Be Just!" But, before the process can be completed, the Harrow breaks apart and, in a final paroxysm, drives a great iron spike into the officer's forehead.

Knives turned against himself or others are, as we have seen, a recurring theme in the diaries and correspondence, as well as in *The Trial* and "Fratricide." That preoccupation extends to the infliction and endurance of pain. Attempting to explain his ghoulish interest in the abscess under Felice's bridge and its breaking up piecemeal, Kafka wrote to Grete:

> Don't you get pleasure out of exaggerating painful things as much as possible? For people with weak instincts it often seems to me the only way to drive out pain; like medicine, which is devoid of all good instincts, it cauterizes the sore spot. By so doing, of course, nothing definite is achieved, but the moment itself—and those with bad and weak instincts haven't time to worry about more than that—almost pleasurable. (*LF*, 331)

Even more striking are his comments to Milena on her translation of an excerpt from Upton Sinclair's novel, *Jimmy Higgins*, which had appeared in a Prague newspaper at the time of their breakup in November 1920. He was manifestly distraught:

> The fact that you chose precisely this passage to translate is a sign that we have similar tastes. Yes, torture is extremely important to me—my sole occupation is torturing and being tortured. Why? For much the same reason as Perkins [a policeman in the novel] and, just as thoughtless, mechanically, and in line with

the tradition; namely to get the damned word out of the damned mouth. I once expressed the stupidity contained in this as follows (it doesn't help at all to recognize the stupidity): "The animal wrests the whip from the master and flails itself in order to become the master, unaware that this is only a fantasy created by a new knot in the master's thong." (*LM*, 214–5)

The punishment in *In the Penal Colony* is no more grotesquely out of proportion with the condemned man's offense than the punishments meted out for more nebulous transgressions in the three works that Kafka had wished Wolff to publish in one volume as *Sons*. *In the Penal Colony* stands out because of the meticulous, graphic descriptions of the Harrow and its operation, which seem to have mesmerized the author. And there is nothing in those other stories as chilling as the relativist position of the distinguished European explorer, who will neither help nor hinder, or what he says to himself when he sees the officer take the condemned man's place in the Harrow:

> If the judicial procedure which the officer cherished were really so near its end—possibly as a result of his own intervention, as to which he felt himself pledged—then the officer was doing the right thing; in his place the explorer would not have acted otherwise. (*LM*, 163)

The explorer is not Kafka, and he doesn't speak for the author. He is a neutral observer, the only one to appear in Kafka's fiction. Kafka's intrinsic and unshakable humanism is as much a factor in the power the Harrow exercises over him as is his troubling fascination with pain. That humanism, and the crystalline hardness of Kafka's writing, lift *In the Penal Colony*, which is a near-masterpiece, high above Octave Mirbeau's fin de siècle kitsch torture novel, *Le jardin des supplices*, an account of a voyager who, in the course of investigating penitential systems in the Far East, relishes a visit to a garden of torture. Mirbeau's novel isn't mentioned in the inventory of Kafka's library, but a consensus exists that it was one of his literary sources. (*Bi*, 57, 278)

In the Penal Colony has been read as an allegory, in which the Old Commandant is Old Testament Jehovah, the commandments inscribed on the bodies of condemned men are the Ten Commandments, and the officer is Moses, because in his leather wallet he brings the Old Commandant's designs of the sentences to be inscribed on backs of condemned men. The new commandant is consequently seen as overturning the harsh old law. Should one then venture that the officer's self-immolation on the Harrow is the analogue of the Crucifixion, and the explorer stands in for Pontius Pilate? It is highly improbable that Kafka intended any such parody of Judaism and Christianity. With considerably more justification, *In the Penal Colony* has also been read as echoing the degradation of Captain Alfred Dreyfus and his confinement, in conditions that were brutal, and to a large extent illegal, and included the shackling of his legs to his bed. The details were recounted in Dreyfus's widely read memoir, *Cinq années de ma vie 1894–1899*, published in 1901.

Dreyfus was a French artillery captain serving on temporary assignment with the army general staff. He was the only Jewish officer in that position, the general staff by custom excluding Jews. In October 1894, on the basis of trumped-up evidence, Dreyfus was accused of delivering military secrets to the German embassy. Two months later, he was convicted of treason by a military tribunal and deported in perpetuity to Devil's Island. In due course the documentary evidence and the testimony of

Dreyfus's brother officers, who had conspired against him, unraveled. In 1899, he received a presidential pardon; in 1906, the highest court in France overturned the judgments of the two military tribunals that had condemned him and declared his innocence. The revelation of the extent and virulence of anti-Semitism in the officer corps and high command of the French army, and indeed in all strata of French society, and the graphic details of the punishment to which Dreyfus had been subjected, shocked and frightened Jews everywhere. If Jews were so vulnerable in republican France, the first European country to emancipate them, where could they find safety?

At the time of his book's publication, and for years thereafter, Dreyfus may have been the most famous man in Europe. The memoir does not appear in the inventory of Kafka's library, but he likely read it. He would have almost certainly heard it discussed, and may have recalled it at the time he was writing *In the Penal Colony.* A specific trace of Devil's Island in Kafka's text may be that the officer speaks French (but curiously, as we will see, so does the schoolteacher in *The Castle*), although neither the soldier guarding the condemned man or the condemned man himself understand that language. The wrong done to Dreyfus and the wrong about to be done to the condemned soldier converge, in that both Dreyfus and the soldier have been denied basic legal rights: in Kafka's colony, guilt is never to be doubted; the soldier has not had opportunity to defend himself, and he has not even been told of the sentence imposed on him. What's more, the presumption of guilt recalls the attitude of many superior officers on the French general staff who fervently believed that, as a Jew, Dreyfus was by heredity predisposed to commit treason.

However, the Dreyfus Case was not about torture or even the nature of the punishment the military tribunal imposed. Deportation in perpetuity as punishment for treason would have been accepted by French society and doubtless by Dreyfus himself as an appropriate sentence, capital punishment in treason cases having been abolished, provided there was no doubt about guilt. Indeed, the fact that Dreyfus would not be executed was initially greeted by outrage. At the heart of the case, and the reason for the furor it provoked, was a legal scandal: the conviction of an innocent man on the basis of fraudulent evidence, the most telling parts of which were presented to the military tribunal in secret, so that neither the accused nor his lawyer could exercise the defendant's basic right to examine and challenge documents and testimony. Of course, once the misconduct of the minister of war, the general staff, and the prosecutor came to light, the extraordinarily harsh treatment of Dreyfus resulted in an outpouring of sympathy for the victim and outrage against his jailors.

But there is no suggestion that Kafka wanted the reader to doubt that the soldier had indeed been insubordinate, and neither the Austro-Hungarian nor the German army of the time would have tolerated a soldier's yelling at an officer "Throw that whip away or I'll eat you alive," even if the soldier had been lashed across the face. (*CS*, 146) Much more likely, whether or not Kafka had been thinking of Captain Dreyfus, he was expressing his general loathing for the severity if not cruelty of punishments meted out by military tribunals as well as other criminal law courts, whether the condemned man is guilty as charged or innocent.

Let us assume that, as is very likely, Kafka had in mind Devil's Island; Jehovah's angry and vindictive character and the inordinately cruel punishments and unfair trials he has inflicted on his people (the Flood, the burning of Sodom and Gomorrah together with their inhabitants, barring Moses from the Promised Land, and ordering Abraham to sacrifice Isaac being but a few examples); and the barbaric aspects of military discipline. That doesn't

mean that we should open *In the Penal Colony* and say
to ourselves: now we will read about Dreyfus and Devil's
Island, or the failure of theodicy, or the barbaric aspects
of military codes of justice. We should take the story for
what it is—the author's desperately brave attempt to work
through nightmares from which he could not awake—with
the nimbus of all possible associations and references that
surrounds the story serving to enhance our experience and
not to dictate an interpretation. The truth is that writers
of fiction very seldom—perhaps never—think of only one
experience, or one concept, or only one person or group
of persons, when they create a work of fiction, even if it is
a *roman à clef*, which is not the case of anything written
by Kafka. If a work is on track, its creator is assailed by a
multitude of nascent possibilities most of which he doesn't
pursue. Unexpected insights, some very useful, become
miraculously available.

An entry dated September 23, 1912, which in the diary
follows directly after the text of "The Judgment," records
Kafka's experience of that process:

> Many emotions carried along in the writing, joy, for
> example, that I shall have something beautiful for
> Max's *Arkadia* [a periodical edited by Brod], thoughts
> about Freud, of course; in one passage of *Arnold Beer* [a
> novel by Brod about "the Jewish Question"]; in another,
> of Wassermann [Austrian writer, Jakob Wassermann
> (1873–1934], in one, of Werfel's giantess [Werfel's
> novel, *Die Riesin*]; of course, also of my 'Urban World'
> [a fragment composed in 1911, possibly the prototype
> of "The Judgment" (*D*, 40)]. (*D*, 213)

There may be a residue of that joy and those thoughts in
"The Judgment," but by the end of the September night of
wonders they had been changed, together with all the other

resources Kafka used in his story, "into something rich and strange," which was the completed short story, pitting a son against a ruthless and omnipotent father.

The son, Georg Bendemann, a young businessman, sits in his own pleasant room on a Sunday morning and gazes out the window at the river, the bridge, and distant hills beyond the far bank. He has just finished a letter to an old friend, who had "actually run away to Russia some years before, being dissatisfied with his prospects at home." (*CS*, 77) Success has eluded him there as well. Writing to him hasn't been an easy task because Georg senses that the disparity between his own well-being and financial comfort and the friend's situation has grown so great that it may incite the friend to envy. Moreover, until that very morning he had held off disclosing his own engagement to a "Fräulein Frieda Brandenfeld, a girl from a well-to-do family." By contrast, the friend, who has no intercourse with the colony of his own countrymen in St. Petersburg, or with Russian families, has had to resign himself to the life of an old bachelor.

In the course of these after-breakfast ruminations we also learn that Georg's mother had died a couple of years earlier, that he and his widowed father are sharing the household, and that "since her death his father had become less aggressive, although he was still active in the business." (*CS*, 78) Also since the mother's death Georg "had applied himself with greater determination to the business as well as everything else. (*CS*, 78) Whether as a result of that increased effort or by chance, the family business has prospered in a most unexpected way. The letter finished, he puts it into his pocket and goes to his father's room, just across the hall. He hadn't entered that room for months, but he and his father see each other daily at business, and over the midday meal they both take at eating houses. In the evening, even if Georg is going out, they sit together in the living room for a while, reading papers.

The appearance of his father's room startles Georg: it is so dark even on this sunny morning; the remains of breakfast, not much of which has been eaten, haven't been removed by the maid; the father is sitting, in an incongruously heavy dressing gown, in a corner of the room hung with mementoes of his late wife. When the father gets up, Georg remarks to himself that his father is still "a giant of a man." (*CS*, 81) So far so good. We could be in an end-of-nineteenth-century Chekhov or Maupassant story, and the only surprise is that the author is Kafka, who had never written anything of the sort before. But "The Judgment" is the story which he said "came out of me like a real birth, covered with filth and slime, and only I have the hand that can reach to the body itself and the strength of desire to do so." (*D*, 214) Without warning, the mood and the tempo of the story change. When Georg tells his father that he has finally written the letter to his St. Petersburg friend about the engagement, the father accuses him of not telling the whole truth. There are many things in the business he doesn't know about, he complains, perhaps done behind his back; he can't tell because his memory has been failing. Then he adds very gently:

> about this letter, I beg you, Georg, don't deceive me. It's a trivial affair, it's hardly worth mentioning, so don't deceive me. Do you really have this friend in St. Petersburg? (*CS*, 82)

Anyone who has been responsible for an aged parent will recognize the feelings of embarrassment and guilt, and something close to panic, that sweep over Georg. So the old man has begun to lose his mind! Of course, he assures the father that he would never tell a fib, that he can't do without him in business, that the father must be given for his personal use the sitting room which receives plenty of light—and, resolving to send for the doctor, he tries to get him to bed. It's no use. The father insists that Georg has no friend in St. Petersburg; he's pulling his father's leg.

Nonetheless, Georg gets his father ready for bed, in the process noticing that his underwear is soiled, carries him there in his arms, and tucks him in. Thereupon a most peculiar exchange takes place. Am I well covered up? the father asks. Georg assures him that he is, and right away the father goes on the attack. He throws off the blankets and springs erect, only one hand touching the ceiling. "You wanted to cover me up," he cries, "but I'm far from being covered up." Vitriol flows as the father explains that he has had a continuous correspondence with the St. Petersburg friend—who "would have been a son after my heart." (*CS*, 85) But Georg has betrayed his friend. And only now that he thinks he can "sit on [his father] and he wouldn't move, then my fine son makes up his mind to get married." (*CS*, 85) And that is not all:

> "Because she lifted up her skirts," his father began to flute, "because she lifted her skirts like this, the nasty creature," and mimicking her he lifted his shirt so high one could see the scar on his thigh from his war wound, "because she lifted her skirts like this and this you made up to her, and in order to make free with her undisturbed you have disgraced your mother's memory, betrayed your friend, and stuck your father into bed so that he can't move. But he can move, or can't he?"
>
> And he stood up quite unsupported and kicked his legs out. His insight made him radiant. (*CS*, 85)

We have seen almost the same language the *Letter to His Father* written in 1919, coupled with his father's offer to take Franz to a brothel as an alternative to marriage, thrown back in his father's face when Kafka recalled the tongue-lashing to which he had been subjected because of his engagement to Julie Wohryzek. Was this a case of life imitating art, seven years later? Had Kafka put those words consciously or unconsciously into his father's mouth because his great 1912 story was still so present in his mind? Or is it possible that this form of unbearably vulgar insult was standard diction among Prague Jews of Herman Kafka's vintage and paper-thin civilization? It is impossible to tell. There is not a clue to be found in Kafka's diaries or letters.

Georg recognizes the force of the onslaught and shrinks into a corner. A long time ago he had made up his mind to watch even the least of his father's movements, so as not to be surprised. "At this moment he recalled this long-forgotten resolve and forgot it again, like a man drawing a short thread through the eye of a needle." A magnificent sentence: it signals Georg's doom. The tirades continue. The father's resentments spill out, as if from an overflowing sewer, until at last he cries:

> "An innocent child, yes, that you were, truly, but still more truly you have been a devilish human being!—And therefore take note: I sentence you to death by drowning!" (*CS*, 87)

Remember, we are in Kafka reality. Instead of getting the doctor to inject the old fool with a sedative, Georg flees from the room. Rushing downstairs, he meets the cleaning woman. "Jesus!" she cries, and covers her face with her apron, but he is already gone. On he rushes, across the roadway and onto the bridge "grasping at the railings as a starving man clutches food." (*CS*, 88) Like the distinguished gymnast he had once been in his youth, to his parents' pride, he swings himself over the railings and, when a bus comes that will cover with the roar of its motor the noise of the splash, he exclaims "Dear parents, I have always loved you, all the same," and lets himself drop. (*CS*, 88)

A death sentence has been imposed and carried out, but for what crime? Georg's having been too pushy in running the business after his father had stepped back? Neglect of the father? Neglect of the St. Petersburg friend? None of these seem right. What sets the father off must be the mention of the engagement, and it is when the father raves about the fiancée that the tirade reaches the high C. So the offense must have consisted in the son's decision to have a sexual life, and potentially become a father himself. Chronos, the primeval god, devoured his children without regard to gender or guilt until his son Zeus killed him. Zeus was helped by Rhea, his mother and Chronos's wife and sister. No one helps Georg; in Kafka's world, Georg's mother, if alive, would have at times moderated his father's bursts of temper but her essential unity with the father would have been entire. Kafka's fathers banish or kill sons who transgress. The sons do not fight back. They do not all, like Georg, rush to become their own executioners, but, without exception, they submit to the punishment.

The first sentence of *The Metamorphosis*—"As Gregor Samsa awoke one morning from uneasy sleep he found himself transformed in his bed into a gigantic insect"—reads like the beginning of a fairy tale; but it's a fairy tale without a princess or good fairy to break the evil spell. (*CS*, 89) Gregor isn't astonished by what has happened to him, and at first misjudges its implications. As an overworked traveling salesman, he is appalled to have overslept, although the alarm clock had been set as usual to go off at four. It's now quarter of seven. He has missed his regular five o'clock train. What's more, he still needs to pack up his samples. All the same, he thinks that if he really hurries he can catch the seven o'clock. But how to hurry with the insect body and its many thin legs that he hasn't gotten used to? He doesn't even know how to get out of bed. And how can he leave his room? He has locked the three doors leading to it, out of habit acquired in the countless hotels where most of his nights have been spent. As he soon discovers, opening a locked door is an arduous and painful task for a beetle. He must first make himself fall out of bed, then hoist his body into a vertical position against the door, and, finally, use his soft and vulnerable mouth to turn the key. Gregor has been successful as a commercial traveler, but he hasn't been happy. It's an occupation he chose after his father failed in business, thinking it more likely than an office job to enable him to support his parents and his lovely younger sister Grete. His feelings for her are both paternal and slightly incestuous, consistent with Kafka's take on such matters: "Love between brother and sister—the repeating of the love between mother and father." (*D*, 210) Gregor knows it will take another five or six years to pay the father's debts. That's a long time. It occurs to him that it might be a good thing for him to be fired right now—who knows?

The remaining three months of Gregor's life as a beetle are a Golgotha. He frightens and repels even Grete and his mother. Since he understands that when Grete comes to feed him she can't bear to look at him, he hides tactfully under the sofa. The only foods he will eat are scrapings of the garbage pail. He emits an odor so foul that Grete rushes to open the window as soon as she enters his room. Being capable only of beetle noises, he cannot make himself understood when he tries to speak. His vision changes: the building across the street from his room, at which he had been used to stare, has become an indistinct smudge.

The sticky stuff on the soles of his feet makes it possible for him to crisscross walls and hang upside down from the ceiling, but it leaves ugly stains. This form of recreation gives Grete an unfortunate idea. With her mother's help she attempts to empty his room entirely, to give him more space in which to crawl around. He is sad to have his familiar objects taken away, but he submits, and it is his mother who first formulates an objection. She tells Grete that what they are doing shows that all hope of his return in human form has been abandoned. The remark causes Gregor to decide that he will defend at least one possession: the picture he had recently cut out from an illustrated magazine and put into a pretty frame; it hangs on the wall where he can look at it from his bed. The subject is a lady, with a fur cap and a fur stole, sitting upright and holding out to the spectator a huge fur muff into which the whole of her forearm has disappeared. A picture to make a traveling salesman dream. And so, when Grete tries to remove it, he "quickly crawled up to it and pressed himself to the glass, which was a good surface to hold on to, and comforted his hot belly." (*CS*, 118) His mother faints at the sight and has to be administered smelling salts.

In the ensuing confusion, Gregor escapes to the living room and is confronted there by his father. The old man, who had become "fat and sluggish" after five years of being supported by Gregor, has found work as a messenger at a bank and seems rejuvenated. Tricked out in blue livery, he advances on Gregor. The enormous size of his shoe soles alone is terrifying: to what cruel use will they be put? Gregor remembers that his father had "from the very first day of his new life [as a beetle] . . . believed only the severest measures suitable for dealing with him." (*CS*, 121) As he attempts to run away, the father bombards him with apples taken from a dish on the sideboard. The improvised projectiles sink into the flesh of Gregor's back, causing unbearable pain and eventually crippling him because no one thinks of removing them. While the attack continues, his mother rushes toward his father "in complete union with him—but here Gregor's sight began to fail—with her hands clasped around his father's neck as she begged for her son's life." (*CS*, 122)

From now on everything tends toward Gregor's liquidation. He is so crippled that, like an old invalid, he needs ten long minutes to creep across his room; there is no question of being able to crawl up a wall or gambol on the ceiling. But he is reconciled to his condition, because the family now leaves the door to the living room open for an hour or two in the evening so that he can see them all at the lamp-lit table and listen to their talk. Crushed by work and the presence of the beetle in the next room, they mostly keep silent. After dinner, the mother does fine stitching for an underwear firm, and Grete studies shorthand and French in the hope of advancing in her career as a salesgirl. The father is asleep in his chair, still wearing his uniform. Not brand new to start with, it looks dirty and stained with grease.

The apartment is too large and too expensive for the family's new circumstances, so lodgers are taken in. They are served dinner in the living room; the mother, father, and Grete eat in the kitchen. The three lodgers currently in residence are superb comical creations. All three wear full beards; one is the leader. The other two, who seem to have no independent thoughts or desires, repeat his every word; they are Mutt and Jeff, Bohemian style. Another, much graver, crisis comes to a head while Grete plays her violin for that awful threesome. Gregor, desperately eager to hear her better, limps into the living room:

> And yet just on this occasion he had more reason than ever to hide himself, since, owing to the amount of dust that lay thick in his room and rose into the

air at the slightest movement, he too was covered
with dust; fluff and hair and remnants of food trailed
with him, caught on his back and along his sides; his
indifference to everything was much too great for
him to turn on his back and scrape himself clean on
the carpet, as once he had done several times a day....
Was he an animal, that music had such an effect upon
him? (CS,130)

He resolves to lure Grete with her violin into his room, and
never let her out so long as he lives, for he knows that no one
appreciates her playing as much as he. His frightful appearance
will be useful for the first time; intruders will retreat if he spits
at them. In time, he will reveal to her his secret plan, which
has been to send her, as a student, to the conservatory as soon
as next Christmas. She will be so moved by his decision that
she will burst into tears, and he "would then raise himself to
her shoulder and kiss her on the neck, which now that she
went to business, she kept free of any ribbon or collar." (*CS*,
131) Instead, the lodgers see the beetle and forthwith give
notice. The alliance between Grete and Gregor is broken.
She tells her parents "we must get rid of him ... I don't think
anyone could reproach us in the slightest." (*CS*, 131) The
father agrees. So Gregor's fate is sealed. He makes his way
laboriously to his room, his last glance falling on his mother,
who is almost asleep. The door is pushed shut indignantly by
Grete and locked. In the darkness,

[h]e thought of his family with tenderness and love.
The decision that he must disappear was one that he
held to even more strongly than his sister, if that were
possible. (*CS*, 135)

At daybreak he is dead. He has not only acquiesced in the
sentence passed on him, but, going a step further than Georg

Bendemann, anticipates it as well as carries it out. We realize this when, a little later, the parents, Grete, and the cleaning woman go into Gregor's room, and Grete explains:

> 'It's such a long time since he's eaten anything. The food came out again just as it went in.' Indeed, Gregor's body was completely flat and dry, as could only now be seen when it was no longer supported by the legs and nothing prevented one from looking closely at it. (*CS*, 136–7)

The worst is still to come. While the parents and Grete, having decided to take the day off, are busy writing letters of excuse to their employers, the cleaning woman reappears, giggling amiably, to tell the family that they don't need "to bother about how to get rid of the thing next door. It's been seen to already." She has tossed out the shriveled beetle with the garbage. The announcement "seemed to have shattered again the composure they had barely achieved." (*CS*, 139) But they regain it, and set out by tram for a day of rest and strolls in the country. Comfortably installed, Mr. and Mrs. Samsa notice Grete's increasing vivacity. She has bloomed into a pretty girl with a good figure. It will soon be time to find a husband for her:

> And it was a confirmation of their new dreams and excellent intentions that at the end of their journey their daughter sprang to her feet first and stretched her young body. (*CS*, 137)

A little less than a year after he had completed *The Metamorphosis,* Kafka noted in his diary that he had reread it and found it bad. (*D*, 233) Three months later, he elaborated:

> Great antipathy to "Metamorphosis." Unreadable
> ending. Imperfect almost to its very marrow. It would
> have turned out much better if I had not been inter-
> rupted at the time by a business trip [to Kratzau].
> (*D*, 253)

The "ending" almost certainly refers to the day off that the
Samsa family takes, and not to the description of Gregor's
death. The momentum and logic of the story call for
Gregor to die: there is no other solution. The same cannot
be said of the family outing, and especially the discovery
of Grete's nubility, which may have been intended as a
parody of familial catharsis; instead, it comes off instead as
a superfluous bit of unpleasantness.

What was the nature of Gregor's guilt? And for that
matter, what was his punishment? Was being changed into
a giant beetle part of it, or was the transformation only the
visible symptom of his transgressions? Or was it the natural
consequence of the brutalizing conditions of a traveling
salesman's life and work? One form of transgression might
have been his desire to quit his job as soon as he has paid
off his father's debts, an offense against the work ethic. Is
it grave enough to deserve capital punishment? But there
is another charge to be added to the indictment, Gregor's
venture into the realm of sexuality—a domain reserved
for the father. Hints that this is the case include Gregor's
clinging to the picture of the woman with a fur muff,
his "hot belly" covering it, and his daydreams about "a
chambermaid in one of the rural hotels, a sweet and fleeting
memory, a cashier in a milliner's shop, whom he had wooed
earnestly but too slowly." (*CS*, 125) And gravest of all,
there is that kiss he would have liked to plant on Grete's
neck. Kissing a woman's neck is a gesture full of significance
for Kafka: that is a liberty Joseph K. permits himself in his
first interview with Fräulein Bürstner. But what kind of

moral system must we posit for these trifles to justify the excruciating punishment visited on Gregor? Or a father's battening upon the son's misery? None that Kafka or we could accept. Let the cleaning woman call all she wants upon Jesus when she meets Georg Bendemann in his mad rush down the stairs and to his death by water, and Gregor's mother, seeing the giant beetle, plead "Help, for God's sake, help!" No one hears and no one will answer. Onlookers, if there are any, will prove as indifferent as the explorer in *Penal Colony*, and as unlikely to lend a helping hand.

On the surface, "The Stoker" presents a straightforward case of sexual misconduct followed by prompt and very stern parental reproof. Karl Rossmann, a German-speaking not-quite-sixteen-year-old from Prague, has been packed off to America by his parents because a servant girl had seduced him and has borne his child. The servant girl, who was thirty-five, we later learn, led Karl into her room, locked the door, took off his clothes and hers, and had him lie on her bed. Then

> she lay down by him and wanted some secret from him, but he could tell her none, and she showed anger, either in jest or in earnest, shook him, listened to his heart, offered her breast that he might listen to her in turn, but could not bring him to do it, pressed her naked belly against his body, felt with her hand between his legs, so disgustingly that his head and neck started up from the pillows, then thrust her body several times against him—it was as if she were a part of himself, and for that reason, perhaps, he was seized with a terrible feeling of yearning. With the tears running down his cheeks he reached his own bed at last, after many entreaties from her to come again. (*A*, 29–30)

He is hardly a seducer, but that doesn't seem to matter. Equipped with an umbrella and a traveling box containing a suit, not as good as the one he has on, but recently mended, a piece of salami his mother had packed as an extra tidbit, some shirts, a little money, and a photograph of his parents, he is banished and packed off to America. When the story begins, Karl's ship has just entered New York harbor. He is on deck with his box and in a sudden burst of sunshine he sees the Statue of Liberty: "The arm with the sword rose up as if newly stretched aloft, and round the figure blew the free winds of heaven." (A, 3) Yes, the torch of freedom has been changed into an avenger's weapon. It would be nice to think it was intentional, but almost surely it was a slip of the pen. But the box is in jeopardy. That is because Karl has forgotten his umbrella below in his cabin and leaves the box in care of a stranger, while he goes off in search of an object that most boys his age would have liked to heave overboard at the first opportunity. He is making his way through the labyrinth of the ship's endless corridors and stairs when he meets the ship's stoker, a huge man and, like Karl, a German. The stoker summons Karl into his cabin and invites him to lie down on his bunk. The atmosphere is charged with homoerotic feeling, but on the surface decorum is preserved. All that appears is that Karl has chosen a surrogate father and the stoker a son. The roles are reversed in short order, when Karl becomes the stoker's advocate, seeking redress for him from the ship's captain. The stoker claims that the ship's chief engineer, a Romanian, had treated him unfairly because he, the stoker, is a German. Nothing much would have come of this diversion if one of the gentlemen present in the captain's cabin hadn't been keeping an eye on Karl. He asks the boy's name. Karl identifies himself, whereupon the gentleman reveals that he is none other than his Uncle Jacob. More to the point, he is Senator Edward Jacob, a multimillionaire. How did the senator recognize his nephew? It's the servant girl's doing. She had written to the uncle giving Karl's description and the name of the ship on which he was sailing.

Uncle Jacob having taken Karl under his wing, they say goodbye to the captain and proceed to the launch that awaits them. But as Karl steps on the top rung of the ladder, he bursts into violent sobs, causing the senator to put his hand under Karl's chin, draw him close, and caress him with his other hand. They descend into the launch, and at a sign from the senator, the sailors push off and begin to row at full speed. "The Stoker" ends enigmatically:

> Karl took a more careful look at his uncle, whose knees were almost touching his own, and doubts came into his mind whether this man would ever be able to take the stoker's place. And his uncle evaded his eye and stared at the waves on which their boat was tossing. (*A*, 37)

Having become Karl's adoptive father, Uncle Jacob will follow the example of Karl's natural father, and surprisingly, as well as unjustly, banish the youth. The ostensible reason will be that Karl has disobeyed his uncle. In fact, he has tried to be obedient; at worst he has failed to act in accordance with his uncle's hidden wish, proceeding instead in accordance with instructions the uncle has given. Karl will be banished as well by the redoubtable Mr. Pollunder, into whose arms Uncle Jacob has thrust him, and once more by the wistful hotel Manageress of Hotel Occidental. He will form two more inappropriate and ambiguous attachments, to sinister and thuglike Delamarche and Robinson, whom he meets on the open road. The travails Karl undergoes are of a nature to break his spirit and will, but, true to the

tradition of the picaresque novel, Karl and *Amerika* remains
irresistibly buoyant and optimistic.

Looking back three years after he stopped working on
it, Kafka wrote in his diary:

> Dickens's Copperfield. "The Stoker" a sheer imitation
> of Dickens, the projected novel even more so. The
> story of the box, the boy who delights and charms
> everyone, the menial labor, his sweetheart in the
> country house, the dirty houses, et al., but above all
> the method. It was my intention, as I now see, to write
> a Dickens novel, but enhanced by the sharper lights I
> should have taken from the times and the duller ones
> I should have gotten from myself. (*D*, 388)

Writers' work doesn't always conform to their wishes.
Kafka never got around to giving Karl a girlfriend. Neither
Clara Pollunder, a dominatrix who almost throttles him,
nor the adorable Teresa, the Manageress's assistant who
is probably in love with him, fill that role. And Kafka's
novel turns out to be a universe away from the world of
Peggoty, Mr. Micawber, Steerforth, and David Copperfield
himself. Instead, the bustling vigor and sheer wackiness of
Karl's misadventures bring *Amerika* closest to a novel that
Kafka had died too soon to read: Witold Gombrowicz's
masterpiece, *Ferdydurke*, first published in 1937.

Brod remembered that *Amerika* was the sole work that
Kafka had intended to end on an optimistic note, with
wide-ranging prospects. (*B*, 137) The question of Karl's
ultimate fate nagged at him. In the fall of 1915, with
Amerika and *The Trial* lying unfinished, he wrote in his
diary: "Rossmann and K., the innocent and the guilty, in
the end both executed without distinction, the innocent
with a lighter hand, more pushed aside than struck down."
(*D*, 343–4) The truth is that Kafka didn't know how to

bring his charming novel to a conclusion, perhaps because it is a road novel and as such open-ended.

Even though Kafka stopped working on *The Trial* before the end of January 1915 and considered it unfinished, Brod rightly observed in the "Postscript to the First Edition" that "anyone ignorant of the fact that the author himself intended to go on working at ... [*The Trial*] (he failed to do so because his life entered another phase) would hardly be aware of the gaps." (*T*, 271) Unlike *Amerika* and *The Castle*, *The Trial* has the feel of a novel that has been brought to completion.

1915 had been, indeed, a terrible year for Kafka. He was tormented by the obligation to look after the asbestos factory, a troubled Kafka family investment in an enterprise that Elli's husband, Karl Hermann, was supposed to run but couldn't, having been called up for military service. It plunged Franz into despair: "the thought of the factory is my perpetual Day of Atonement" 1/4/15 (*D*, 325); "I shall not be able to write so long as I have to go to the factory" 1/19/15 (*D*, 326); "The end of writing. When will it catch up with me again?" 1/20/15 (*D*, 327). The disastrous meeting with Felice in Bodenbach took place at the end of January. (*D*, 329–8) "I wear myself out to no purpose," he summed up on Christmas Day 1915, "should be happy if I could write, but don't. Haven't been able to get rid of my headaches lately. I have really wasted my strength away....Always this one principal anguish: If I had gone away in 1912, in full possession of all my forces, with a clear head, not eaten by the strain of keeping down living forces!" (*D*, 353) There is no silver bell that rings to tell the writer that he has finished the novel or short story on which he is working. When he comes to reread what he first thought was a finished product, he may change his mind, deciding that a problem has been left hanging, or, on the contrary, that the narrative has been allowed to ramble past the point at which it should have stopped. It does not seem, therefore, impossible that, if Kafka's spirits had been higher, he might have, instead of adding to it, declared *The Trial* finished, subject to the usual prepublication revisions.

But *The Trial* is not only the most realized of Kafka's novels but also has special resonance for contemporary readers, and since the appearance of an English translation in 1937 has been the text most responsible for the widening renown of Kafka's work. Unsurprisingly, the feeding frenzy of exegetes and other types of Kafka scholars circling around *The Trial* has been intense: one can almost hear scholastic dentures going clack-clack. For readers curious about the extent, variety, and abstruseness of studies devoted to the interpretation of *The Trial*, Hartmut Binder's *Kafka's Handbuch*, a magisterial two-volume compendium of all information about Franz's life and work, is the place to go, even though it has not been revised since its initial publication in 1979, and the production of scholarly literature does not appear to have slowed.

Kafka specialists have read *The Trial* as a cabalistic parable; they have submitted it to exegesis in accordance with formal literary theory concerns (e.g., to what genre does *The Trial* belong?); and they have analyzed it by applying existentialist, Marxist, Freudian, structuralist, and gender theories, among others. The common denominator of all such studies, unforgettably lumped together by Milan Kundera under the rubric of Kafkology, is the near-total disregard of the aesthetic aspect of the work, and the effort and space devoted to comments on and rebuttals of other scholars' theories. As such, they seem irrelevant to the general reader, even a reader hardy enough to penetrate the academic jargon. A subgroup of Kafka critics argue, based on Kafka's diary and correspondence, that *The Trial* is a confession, a metaphoric representation of the real life "other trial," namely the confrontation that took place at the Askanische Hof and resulted in the breakup of Kafka's first official engagement to Felice. Since readers are all too often tempted to look in fiction for the autobiography of the author, a brief look at the claims of this branch of Kafkology seems unavoidable.

Two entries in Kafka's diary and a letter Kafka wrote to Grete are invariably adduced in evidence. The first is the entry, referred to earlier, about the reception celebrating the official engagement that had taken place at the apartment of the Bauer parents five days earlier:

> Back from Berlin. Was tied hand and foot like a crimi-
> nal. Had they sat me down in a corner bound in real
> chains, placed policemen in front of me, and let me
> look on simply like that, it could not have been worse.
> And that was my engagement...(*D*, 275)

The second is about the fateful meeting at the Askanische Hof, on July 12. As we have seen, there were present in the hotel room, in addition to Kafka and Felice, Felice's sister Erna, Grete Bloch, and perhaps Dr. Ernst Weiss as well. The next day, Kafka left with Weiss and Weiss's mistress on a vacation that had been planned in advance. While at one of the Baltic resorts the trio visited, he wrote the following in his diary:

> The tribunal in the hotel. Trip in the cab. F.'s face.
> She patted her hair with her hand, wiped her nose,
> yawned. Suddenly she gathered herself together and
> said very studied, hostile things she had long been
> saving up. The trip back with Fräulein Bloch....At
> her [Felice's] parents'. Her mother's occasional tears.
> I recited my lesson. Her father understood the thing
> from every side. Made a special trip from Malmö to
> see me, traveled all night; sat there in his shirtsleeves.

They agreed that I was right, there was nothing, or not much that could be said against me. Devilish in my innocence. Fräulein Bloch's apparent guilt. (*D*, 293)

The third basic element of the proof is a letter to Grete, written on October 15. It is cold and formal. One senses Kafka's fury. He rejected assertions that Grete apparently had made in her letter to him (which has been lost like all the others) concerning Felice's point of view on why the engagement had been broken, and told Grete that nonetheless she was free to continue to write to him although "[i]t's true that at the Askanische Hof you sat in judgment over me ..." (*LF*, 436) Beyond these specific quotations, the proponents of the biographical hypothesis seek support in Kafka's generalized feelings of guilt about the part he had played in the breakup with Felice. They are recorded in his diary and letters to Brod, and seem genuine, however relieved—if not joyous—Kafka may have been to know that the engagement was over, and he had regained his freedom.

The real issue is not whether an autobiographical confession can be coaxed out of *The Trial*. Instead, it is whether looking at the novel through that prism enriches the text and enables the reader to discover in it a new intelligent meaning. The opposite is true: reading *The Trial* as a variation on the theme of the Askanische Hof encounter trivializes the novel. In that construct, Joseph K., of course, is Kafka, and Fräulein Bürstner, the typist whose room is across Frau Grumbach's living room from K.'s, turns into Felice (Felice's initials F.B. recall Fräulein Bürstner, and in addition Felice's first job was as a typist); the scene in K.'s and Fräulein Bürstner's rooms in the course of which K. is arrested, but left free to go to his work at the bank and otherwise carry on with his business, becomes the analogue of the official engagement following which Kafka remained free to return to Prague; and K.'s execution equals the July 12 scene at the Askanische Hof. Finding room for Herman Kafka in *The Trial* is difficult: like *The Castle*, it is a novel without a father figure. But perhaps that doesn't matter; Herman's role in the Askanische Hof debacle was minimal unless we go back to the beginning of time and adduce the damage he did to his son's psyche. The suggestion that Joseph K.'s bumbling busybody of an uncle, who comes in from the country and introduces K. to Advocate Huld, may be a stand-in for Herman Kafka is particularly unconvincing. Kafka venerated and loathed his father as an oversized, powerful, intellectually dominating, and brutally efficient figure. The uncle is all but that.

Adepts of the biographical theory do not rest their case on transpositions of roles, coincidences, and the like; they also point to Kafka's torment over having induced Felice to accept his marriage proposal when he knew deep inside that the union was impossible for him. Kafka's feelings of guilt were sincere, if overdramatized, as for instance in the following diary entry:

> My relation to her family has a consistent meaning only if I conceive myself as its ruin.... I have made F. unhappy, weakened the resistance of all those who need her so much now, contributed to the death of her father, come between Felice and Erna [Felice's sister]....(*D*, 319)

Such feelings were, however, but one element of Kafka's vast and undifferentiated sense of culpability and inadequacy. Its sources were unrelated to the broken engagement and lay deeper. Similarly, the humiliation suffered in the course of the proceedings at the Askanische Hof mingled with direct and vicarious experience of other humiliations and punishments, all of them likewise involving trials: the Tiszaeszláer, Hilsner, Beilis, and, of course, Dreyfus affairs.

It is nonetheless possible that the incident at the Askanische Hof in some sense jump-started *The Trial*—perhaps even inspired its title, since Kafka referred in his diary to the "tribunal in the hotel." On the other hand, he also used the word "trial" tellingly five years later in another context, referring in the *Letter* to "this terrible trial that is pending between us [Kafka and his sisters] and you [their father]." (*S*, 142) Perhaps that word is always on a lawyer's lips. Kafka may also have found it amusing to scatter clues hinting at a Felice connection. For instance, in the description of Fräulein Bürstner's room there is a white blouse like Felice's dangling from the latch of the open window. Fräulein Bürstner's lame friend, Fräulein Montag, who confronts K. as the young woman's emissary, was perhaps introduced because Kafka wanted to thumb his nose at Grete Bloch. But whatever shards of Kafka's biography an assiduous search through the novel might reveal, they will not add up to anything of significance or open a new level of understanding. *The Trial* is not about Felice or Grete Bloch or Kafka's courtship of Felice, but about an ordeal the nature and implications of which have no common measure with "Kafka's other trial."

There is an anomalous reason for the special appeal of *The Trial* to contemporary readers. Benito Mussolini, born in the same year as Kafka, became Italy's prime minister in 1922. In 1925, one year after Kafka's death, he dissolved all political parties in Italy and assumed dictatorial powers. Hitler staged his unsuccessful Munich Putsch in the evening of November 8, 1923. At the time, Kafka was living with Dora Diamant in Berlin, itself the scene of violent conflicts between armed gangs of extremists of the left and the right. Kafka remarked on the street brawls, but not the Putsch; in a letter to Brod written in Berlin toward the end of

October 1923, he spoke of the poison he was absorbing from front pages of newspapers, which was more than he could bear, and of the talk of confrontations in the city. (*L*, 388) Charged with treason, Hitler was imprisoned for nine months in the fortress of Landsberg am Lech, and used his time there to write *Mein Kampf*, the first volume of which was published in 1925. In April 1917, Germany allowed Lenin to travel in a sealed wagon from Zurich to St. Petersburg's Finland Station, a portentous initiative with consequences that included the rise of the Soviet totalitarian state and thus went far beyond the intended result, which was to interfere, by fomenting social unrest, with Russia's ability to continue to wage war.

The Trial, with its celebrated first sentence—"Someone must have been telling lies about Joseph K., for without having done anything wrong he was arrested one fine morning—" and the proceedings against K. under a secret legal system, seems so clearly to prefigure life under twentieth-century totalitarian regimes with their secret laws and police state terror that inevitably readers have wondered about Kafka's insight into history and politics. Could this novel, published in 1925 but written during the fall of 1914 and January 1915, therefore before the seminal events of Bolshevik, Fascist, and Nazi rule, have been a veiled prophecy? Had the apolitical and withdrawn author foreseen the coming of a catastrophe that was still invisible to great statesmen? Nothing in Kafka's diaries, or correspondence, or in the recollections of his friends, suggests that such was the case. The answer must be that Kafka's vision, which was only of things as they were, turned out to be eerily congruous with the reality of the near future. The ample materials that went into fashioning it included: his experience as a Habsburg subject, and as a trainee at the Prague Court, with the empire's sclerotic, but still all-powerful bureaucracy and its labyrinthine

"Kafkaesque" ways; intimate knowledge of the Insurance Institute's own bureaucracy and arcane regulations; dealing with victims of industrial accidents whose claims came before him, and against whom he was at times obliged to litigate; virulent and ubiquitous Czech anti-Semitism that taught him unforgettable lessons on the meaning of being rejected and despised by one's neighbors; and, of course, everything for which he reproached his father—his brutality, capriciousness, and injustice.

Not to be forgotten in this connection is the hapless "Good Soldier Schwejk," the celebrated antihero of Jaroslav Hašek's eponymous novel, published in 1923, which relates the misadventures during the Great War of a soldier in the Austro-Hungarian army. By an ironic coincidence, Hašek was born the same year as Kafka, and died of tuberculosis in Prague in 1923. Schwejk and Joseph K., the creations of these two Prague authors, could have been twins separated at birth. There is no indication that Kafka had read Hašek's novel, but Hašek's perception of the Austro-Hungarian bureaucracy and army as a sinister as well as ludicrous Rube Goldberg contraption was part of the zeitgeist; it pervades novels as different from *The Trial* and *Schwejk* as Robert Musil's, *Man Without Qualities*, the first two volumes of which were published only in 1930 and 1932, and Joseph Roth's *Radetsky March*, also published in 1932. As we shall see, the absurdities of that bureaucracy are also mirrored in the maniacal chicaneries of Count Westwest's administration in *The Castle*.

Since Kafka was not a prophet, reading *The Trial* as a parable about totalitarianism cannot reveal anything he had intended to say about it, or, for example, the rule of law. That was not his subject. The situation is different when we take away from *Macbeth* or *Henry IV, Part I* lessons that we then apply to the conduct of contemporary political leaders, since the use and abuse of power was exactly what

Shakespeare was writing about. As we read *The Trial* we can, however, inventory the ways Joseph K.'s fate could be our own if we were to fall into the hands of the secret police or intelligence services of some readily imaginable state.

Kafka enjoyed reading from his own works and laughing at his own humor even when it verged on the macabre. Brod recalled how:

> [W]e friends of his laughed quite immoderately when he first let us hear the first chapter of *The Trial*. And he himself laughed so much that there were moments when he couldn't read any further. Astonishing enough, when you think of the fearful earnestness of this chapter. (*B*, 178)

In a similar vein, three months after finishing *The Metamorphosis*, Kafka wrote to Felice about having spent a pleasant evening at Brod's. "I read myself into a frenzy with my story. But then we did let ourselves go, and laughed a lot." (*LF*, 209) No wonder: laughing through tears is a Central European specialty, and the works from which Kafka was reading are unsurpassed satires of petit bourgeois life in Prague.

The best example of how closely comedy and despair cohabit in Kafka's fiction may be "A Report to the Academy," a deadpan, ostensibly self-congratulatory address delivered by a large ape dressed up as a human being on the circumstances of his capture in the wild and subsequent training that have brought him to his present high state of accomplishment. (*CS*, 250) Nothing could be more hilarious or devastatingly sad. Caught in the jungle, wounded, named Red Peter by reason of a scar on his cheek left by a bullet wound, locked up in a cage on board a ship, plied with liquor by sailors, confronted by the choice between a cage in a zoo and life as an artist, the ape chose to become a performer, and so has reached his present exalted status:

With an effort which up till now has never been repeated I managed to reach the cultural level of an average European. In itself that might be nothing to speak of, but it is something insofar as it has helped me out of my cage and opened a special way out for me, the way of humanity....There was nothing else for me to do, provided always that freedom was not to be my choice. (*CS*, 258)

Having made the rational choice, this most articulate of autodidacts finds his wishes not only fulfilled but also anticipated:

When I come home from banquets, from scientific receptions, from social gatherings, there sits waiting for me a half-trained little chimpanzee and I take comfort from her as apes do. By day I cannot bear to see her: for she has the insane look of the bewildered half-broken animal in her eye; no one else sees it, but I do, and I cannot bear it. (*CS*, 259)

All the misery and scandal of circuses and zoos and our mistreatment of animals are have been encapsulated in this short story. Whether it makes us chuckle or weep or laugh through tears depends on our disposition, which is surely what Kafka intended.

Red Peter is a convincing personage. We read the account he gives of himself and forget that apes, however gifted, do not deliver speeches before learned societies. But sooner or later our thoughts will turn to what his words demonstrate: the vast shame of our abuse of animals. We may also think of man's cruelty to other men (*lupus est homo homini*, as Plautus observed more than two thousand years ago), or ponder specific examples: white men's conduct in African colonies, including the slave trade (transacted by Arabs and black kings and chiefs more extensively than by whites); the methods used on behalf of King Leopold of Belgium in exploiting the riches of the Congo, which was his private property; or Spaniards' activities in the New World, with particular stress on the educational efforts of Catholic missionaries who tortured and burned natives at the stake in order to teach them the love of Jesus Christ the Savior. Looking in a different direction, it has been argued persuasively that Kafka intended Red Peter's plight to be a metaphor representing the failure of Jewish assimilation: the effort of Jews persecuted and tormented everywhere giving up the faith and traditions of their fathers and making an immense effort to mimic goyim, which eventually brought them nothing or very little. Each of these ways of thinking of the story is instructive and appropriate, provided we remember that they are not mutually exclusive, so that we do not turn a searing statement about man's inhumanity—but isn't man's humanity the synonym of his inhumanity?—into something needlessly narrower, such as an animal-rights tract, or a summons to Jews to reclaim their authentic identity. As Walter Benjamin, one of Kafka's early unconditional admirers and most astute critics, observed in 1934,

> Kafka had a rare capacity for creating parables for himself. Yet his parables are never exhausted by what is explainable; on the contrary, he took all conceivable precautions against the interpretation of his writings. One has to find one's way in them circumspectly, cautiously, and warily. (*Ill*, 124)

Similar in this to "The Judgment," *The Trial* is a novel with one foot in the nineteenth-century realist tradition. As first-time readers of the opening chapter, we might well think that we were entering a fictional world not unlike those of Gogol, Dostoevsky, and Flaubert. That impression dissipates as we read on: we become aware that behind the minutely described decors and events a force operates that distorts them and creates a counter reality. At the counter reality's center are the special courts, unknown to K. and the constitution and published law in K.'s country. Practically everyone else, however, appears to be in on the secret: Frau Grubach and Fräulein Bürstner; the three clerks who work at K.'s bank; K.'s uncle; and the manufacturing client of the bank K. who directs K. to the painter Titorelli. That is without counting those who are peripheral employees of the courts, such as the washerwoman and her husband, and those who are involved in the court's business: Advocate Huld and his nurse and housekeeper Leni, and the merchant Block, whose case is also pending before the court. K.'s naïveté and ignorance are truly astounding.

The hypnotic power of *The Trial* and its hold on the reader derive in large measure from the tension between that counter reality and the pitch-perfect rendition of K.'s utterly banal existence. K. is an ambitious mid-level bank employee: he lives at a family boardinghouse of not very high order (otherwise how could Fräulein Bürstner or Fräulein Montag afford it?), at which the landlady spends her evenings darning socks and apparently lets her nephew, the Captain, sleep on a sofa in the living room onto which at least some boarders' rooms (among them K.'s and Fräulein Bürstner's) open. His social life is equally empty: unless he has an invitation from the Manager of the bank, after work he usually takes a short walk alone or with colleagues, and then stops at the beer hall where he sits with some older, regular diners at the *Stammtisch*. His connections with family have atrophied. For sex he visits once a week a certain cabaret waitress, who spends her days in bed receiving gentlemen friends such as he. He is distant both from the uncle who was his guardian and from the uncle's daughter. And he is culturally shallow: his Italian is vestigial, his knowledge of the cathedral in his own hometown scant. K.'s character is delineated with the same sharp precision. He is unsure of himself. Why would he otherwise accept so meekly the existence of that unknown court without known foundation in his country's law and constitutions?

His behavior with the Deputy Manager is a mixture of apprehension, envy, and ill will; his treatment of the bank's valued clients is inexcusable; it doesn't occur to him to put their needs ahead of his own, which in good conscience he should. Like most people unsure of themselves, he is harsh with inferiors (his behavior with the Rosencrantz and Guildenstern-like trio of junior bank clerks and the washerwoman wife of a Court usher—until he realizes that she may be useful to him—are random examples). He is vindictive (he blocks the promotion of one of the clerks, he toys with the thought of getting all three fired). The fits of bad temper, turning at times into rage, whether directed at Frau Grubach or at the hearing magistrate, make one question his sanity. Is it possible that an emotionally balanced thirty-year-old would permit himself such outbursts, or such brutality, in dealings with Advocate Huld's client Block and old Huld himself? At such times, among protagonists in fiction, only the nameless first-person narrator of Dostoevsky's *Notes from Underground* seems more loutish and deranged.

K.'s relations with women deserve particular attention. They are attracted to K., perhaps because he is under arrest. Advocate Huld indicates that this is so. Speaking of his maid Leni, he tells K. that she in fact has the peculiarity of finding all accused men attractive. The Advocate affirms that it's almost a "natural law." Leni offers herself to K. upon his first visit, and gives him a key to the lawyer's house so he can visit her whenever he wishes. The washerwoman wife of the Court usher also throws herself at him, and one supposes that he could have had his way with one or more of the little girls who swarm around the painter Titorelli's studio. But, with the exception of Fräulein Bürstner, he is drawn to them only if the requisite "something slightly disgusting"—perhaps analogous to the indispensable element of *toucha*, sexual desire, that Kafka would write about to Milena (*LM*, 146–7) six years later—is present. K. is attracted to the subhuman, the misshapen, and outcast, as signaled by Leni's web fingers, which ally her with the animal world; the washerwoman's profligacy with the judge of the Court and his bowlegged student; even by the lascivious, "prematurely debauched" girls swarming in Titorelli's studio and over the stairs leading to it. His cabaret waitress Elsa has that element because she sells sex. K. is no stranger to dirty thoughts: after the student carries the washerwoman off to the Magistrate, fondling her on the way, K. imagines taking him to visit Elsa and watching him beg on his knees for favors. K. does not become attached to any of these women. Their potential usefulness is all that counts. But there is a strong warning sign implicit in this story, in which everything turns against K., that these women are like figures of lust that tempt a pilgrim or knight on his quest and divert him dangerously from his purpose. The prison chaplain suggests as much to K.: "You cast about too much for outside help... especially from women. Don't you see that it isn't the right kind of help?" (*T*, 211)

Fräulein Bürstner is a special case. It is K. who is drawn to her, perhaps aroused by seeing the Inspector make free with the matchbox on her night table and the bank clerks fiddle with her photographs, which suggest that she too may be soiled, or susceptible to violation. Perhaps the sight of that white blouse sends him a signal. Or is it Frau Grubach's telling him that Fräulein Bürstner has gone to the theater and won't be coming home until late, and the young working woman's moist fatigue when he waylays her? When she does appear, and K. has talked her into letting him come into her room, and has told her about the Court of Inquiry having sat in his room to interrogate him, she remarks that "a court of law has a curious attraction," and goes on to tell him that next month she will begin working at a lawyer's office. Immediately, K. begins to enlist her as a helper in his case. There follows a scene in which K. uses every wile of which he is capable—there aren't many—to come physically closer to her, until he

> seized her, and kissed her first on the lips, then all over the face, like some thirsty animal lapping greedily at a spring of long-sought fresh water. Finally he kissed her on the neck, right on the throat, and kept his lips there for a long time. A slight noise from the Captain's room made him look up. "I'm going now," he said; he wanted to call Fräulein Bürstner by her first name, but he did not know what it was. She nodded wearily, resigned her hand for him to kiss, and went into her room with down-bent head. Shortly afterwards K. was in his bed. He fell asleep almost at once, but before doing so he thought for a little about his behavior, he was pleased with it, yet surprised that he was not still more pleased....(*T*, 29–30)

We know that kiss on the neck: it recalls the kiss that Gregor Samsa yearned to plant on his sister's. Kafka's writing is at its most vivid here, superbly dramatic; he needs only a few words to make the scene come so alive that we think we have seen it unfold. Fräulein Bürstner will be back onstage in a crucial and poignant role in the superb last chapter.

The tension in the novel builds. From his visit to the painter Titorelli's studio, Kafka learns that he is within the Court's power and that he cannot hope for a verdict of not guilty—besides, that might not be the most satisfactory result in his case. K. no longer makes light of the Court's proceedings; on the contrary, thinking about them consumes more and more of his time and saps his energy. He dismisses Advocate Huld, or so it would seem at the conclusion of Chapter VIII, which Brod has flagged as unfinished. My own sense of the narrative tells me that whatever else Kafka might have added to the chapter, it is unlikely that K.'s decision to dismiss the lawyer would have been reversed.

At the opening of Chapter IX, "In the Cathedral," K. has just come back from a business trip—he tries to avoid them, because he thinks they give the Assistant Manager an opportunity to discover mistakes he has made—only to be told that he has been chosen to accompany an important Italian client of the Bank on a sightseeing tour of the city. The project will in fact be reduced to a visit to the cathedral; K. will arrive at the cathedral punctually at ten, as agreed, and will wait for the Italian businessman, who never appears. At last, K. decides to leave the cathedral, but a priest, who has taken his place at the side pulpit, calls out in a strong voice: "Joseph K." There follows a hesitation waltz typical of Kafka and K.: had the priest called out a second time, K. would have continued on his way out of the cathedral, but as he hasn't, and since K. believes the priest has observed his turn of head, to disregard the priest "would have been like a childish game of hide-and-seek." (*T*, 209) He therefore approaches the pulpit and acknowledges that he is Joseph K., "thinking how frankly he used to give his name and what a burden it had recently become to him; nowadays people he had never seen before seemed to know his name." (*T*, 209)

In short order he learns that the priest is a prison chaplain, that his case before the Court is going badly, and that he is "held to be guilty." Soon the priest will inform him that he is "deluding himself about the Court," that "in the writing which prefaces the Law that delusion is described thus."

(*T*, 213) He illustrates his meaning by a parable that Kafka allowed to be published as "Before the Law," without any reference to Joseph K. or his trial, in *A Country Doctor* collection of stories.

It is as follows: a country man comes to the gates of the Law and wishes to enter, but the doorkeeper says that at this time he cannot allow it. Since the gate is open the man asks whether he will be able to enter later. The doorkeeper answers that this is possible. Years pass, and the man, although consistently denied admission, has not budged. Finally, as he lies dying, the doorkeeper tells him no one but he could pass through that gate, and now he is going to close it. The priest then explains the parable, in conclusion telling K. that neither the arguments nor the opinions he has just presented, nor the comments on the parable of students of the Law, are binding on K. "You must not pay too much attention to them," he says. "The scriptures are unalterable and the comments often enough merely express the commentators' despair." (*T*, 217) The implicit warning accords with Benjamin's advice about the need for caution as one makes one's way through Kafka's parables. The sense of the priest's own exegesis, which K. grasps with the utmost reluctance, is that the ways of the Court—he is clearly speaking of the last instance of that jurisdiction—and the Law itself cannot be penetrated by the human mind, and do not concern themselves with human notions of justice: "[w]hatever… [the doorkeeper] may seem to us, he is yet a servant of the Law and as such is beyond human judgment." (*T*, 220) K. mulls over these concepts—not unfamiliar in the Judeo-Christian tradition—and tells the priest that he is elevating lying into a "universal principle." But, Kafka comments, that was not K.'s final judgment. Perhaps K. will remember that the priest has also said that he needn't accept as true everything that the doorkeeper says, but "one must only accept it as necessary." (*T*, 120) A show of the glacial indifference of the power that plays with K. like a cat with a mouse is saved for the last. The priest tells him: "The Court wants nothing from you. It receives you when you come and it dismisses you when you go." (*T*, 222)

The end of *The Trial*, which comes in the next chapter, is hauntingly beautiful and terrible. It is the evening before K.'s thirty-first birthday. (K. was arrested one year earlier, in the morning of his thirtieth birthday.) The long travail is over: K. knows that he has been found guilty. Therefore, it should not be surprising that, although he has not been notified that he will be taken away, he is in his room dressed in black, pulling on a pair of new gloves. We aren't told whether the gloves are black, or the butter-colored kind that would have been customary to wear to a wedding or when calling on a young woman to ask first her father and then herself for her hand. Whichever it was, K. has learned his lesson. At the time of K.'s arrest, Warder Franz had found it necessary to instruct him to put on his black suit and threaten him with a thrashing if he didn't. The men who come for him are also dressed for the occasion, in frock coats and top hats. They seem to K. to be a pair of tenth-rate actors; "They want to finish me off cheaply," he says to himself. (*T*, 224) He goes to the window and looks at the street; but this time, unlike the morning of his arrest a year ago, it is not because he is ashamed, but because, as we realize immediately, he hopes that someone will bear witness. But nearly all the windows across the street are dark: at one window only "some babies were playing behind bars, reaching with their little hands toward each other…" (*T*, 224)

K. and the two men set out. Once they are in the street the men use a grip—winding their arms full-length behind him—so that "the three of them were interlocked in a unity that would have brought all three of them down together had one of them been knocked over.…a unity such as can hardly be formed except by lifeless matter." (*T*, 224) They come into a deserted square adorned with flower beds, and K. for the first time forms the intention to resist:

> I'll expend all the strength I have, he thought. Into his mind came a recollection of flies struggling to get away from the fly paper till their little legs are torn off. The gentlemen won't find it easy. (*T*, 225)

But that is when Fräulein Bürstner appears, or someone like her, the resemblance is close, and K. "suddenly realized the futility of resistance." (*T*, 225) The one person who was perhaps on his side may have just let him down. She hasn't even turned her head in his direction. There would be nothing heroic, he thinks, if he were "to snatch at the last appearance of life by struggling." They move on and, curiously, it is he who leads the way, following the young woman, not because he wanted to overtake her or to keep her in sight, but only "that he might not forget the lesson she had brought into his mind." (*T*, 225) One she had brought to mind, but had not taught him. And what is that lesson? Apparently, it is as follows:

> I always wanted to snatch at the world with twenty hands, and not for a very laudable motive either. That was wrong, and am I to show now that not even a year's trial has taught me anything? Are people to say of me that at the beginning of my case I wanted to finish it, and at the end of it I wanted to begin it again. I don't want that to be said. (*T*, 226)

K. sees that she has turned into a side street, "but by this time K. could do without her." They keep marching in harmony, the two men yielding to him. When he stops, they do too, and then the march continues. That is how they come upon a policeman armed with a saber. He has a bushy mustache. The policeman is about to open his mouth, seeing this "not quite harmless-looking group," the men halt, but K. pulls them along and indeed breaks into a run as soon as he is sure the policeman cannot see them. It is a mysterious moment: K. gives up his last chance to break out of the Court's system and rejoin the old, well-understood order.

The trio arrives at a quarry. The moon shines. The men take off K.'s coat, his waistcoat, and finally his shirt, and fold them neatly, "as if they were likely to be used at some time, although perhaps not immediately." (*T*, 227) Then they walk K. around to keep him from being chilled while they look for a good spot. They find one; it's a boulder —the sort of boulder, one supposes, on which Abraham laid down Isaac for the sacrifice—and settle K. on it. A strange ceremony ensues: one of the men draws a "long thin double-edged butcher's knife" from a sheath under his frock coat and tests the cutting edges. Then they pass the knife to each other, and K. perceives that they expect him to seize the knife and plunge it into his breast. But he does not have the mettle of Georg Bendemann or Gregor Samsa. He finds that "he could not completely rise to the occasion, he could not relieve the officials of all their tasks..." (*T*, 228) Just then—one cannot help thinking, miraculously—a window is thrown open, and

a human figure, faint and insubstantial at that height, leaned abruptly far forward and stretched both arms still farther. Who was it? A friend? A good man? Someone who sympathized? Someone who wanted to help? Was it one person only? Or was it mankind? Was help at hand? Were there arguments in his favor that had been overlooked? Of course there must be. Logic is doubtless unshakable, but it cannot withstand a man who wants to go on living. Where was the Judge

> whom he had never seen? Where was the high Court,
> to which he had never penetrated? He raised his hands
> and spread out all of his fingers. (*T*, 228)

Perhaps there was no help; in any event it was too late
to find out. The hands of one of the men were already at
K.'s throat,

> while the other thrust the knife deep into his heart and
> turned it there twice. With failing eyes K. could still see
> the two of them immediately before him, cheek leaning
> against cheek, watching the final act. "Like a dog!"
> he said; it was as if the shame of it must outlive him.
> (*T*, 229)

Suppose there had been "a good man," a representative of
"humanity," to bear witness, would it therefore have been
possible to reach a moral conclusion, for example about
the solidarity of mankind face-to-face with injustice? That
question is best left to each reader.

There are many thematic links between *The Trial* and *The
Castle*, Kafka's complex, cluttered, and heartbreakingly
beautiful last novel. Both protagonists—Joseph K. in the
former, K. in the latter— struggle in a maze that sometimes
seems to have been designed on purpose to thwart and
defeat them. More often, the opposite appears to be true:
there is no purpose; the maze simply exists. Joseph K. seeks
justice: acquittal of the crime, unknown to him, of which he
stands accused. K.'s goal is less certain. *The Castle* is a richer
novel than *The Trial* in narrative breadth, the development
of engaging and unforgettable secondary characters (Frieda,
Olga, Amalia, the landladies of the two village inns, Pepi,
and Bürgel, among others), and descriptions of the nameless
snowbound village and interiors of inns and peasants' huts

that call to mind the paintings of Pieter Bruegel. Had Kafka been able to finish it, or at least bring it closer to completion, *The Castle* would have stood at the pinnacle of his creation. As it is, the reader may occasionally find him- or herself in the same predicament as a character in the Isaac Bashevis Singer story: "I read your Kafka's *Castle*. Interesting, very interesting, but what is he driving at?"

At the center of the novel is a restless and disquieting quest: that of K., a wanderer and a stranger, his identity stripped to a single initial. Having left an unnamed and distant country to which it may not be possible for him to return, he is ostensibly seeking to assume the post of land surveyor for the village, for which position he may or may not have been engaged by the castle authorities. The castle looms over the village where K. has arrived and houses the all-powerful administration at the service of its lord, Count Westwest. If K. had indeed been hired by the castle, it may have been due to a mistake. There is, however, a different version of K.'s quest, offered by him midway through the novel: K. would have liked to arrive in the village unnoticed, without a fuss being made, so that he might find good steady work somewhere as a farmhand. The issue is never settled, and K.'s intentions never become clear. But even the more modest wish would in all likelihood have been denied. The villagers are brutish and hostile: upon arrival he is told that he may not stay in the village even overnight, unless he obtains permission from Count Westwest. The next morning, a silent, slow-witted peasant lays it on the line: there is no custom of hospitality in the village, and guests aren't needed. "'Cause for a slight attack of despair,' was the thought that came to him [K.] upon hearing this, 'if I were only here by accident, not on purpose.'" (*C*, 14) None of the villagers, and probably few of the gentlemen who are members of the administration, have ever seen the Count. Thoughts of the aged and senile Emperor Franz

Josef must have passed through Kafka's mind when he wrote the Count into his novel. The endless paperwork, nighttime interrogations, and other chicaneries with which the gentlemen are occupied are a brilliant send-up of the Austro-Hungarian bureaucracy, the memories of which were obviously as fresh in Kafka's mind in 1922 as they had been in 1914, when he was writing about Joseph K.'s case before the Court and the Court's weird procedures.

Early in *The Castle*, the terms of a paradox are established. On the one hand, a letter from Klamm, the most magnetic and mystifying of the gentlemen, confirms—albeit in ambiguous terms—that K. has been "accepted into the Count's service." On the other, it is made clear that he will never be allowed to come to the castle. Why should he wish to go there, and why the interdiction? These questions, which sometimes seem to be at the core of K.'s story, are left unanswered, just as no reason is given for his having undertaken the arduous journey in the first place, except a vague reference to hard times at home. This being Kafka's reality, we accept it as is. To quote again from Singer's story, "A master does not have to follow the rules." Indeed, if rules accessible to our reason applied to K. there might be no novel. But K.'s behavior, like Joseph K.'s, is highly bizarre, even in the context of Kafka's reality. Every Habsburg subject imbibed with his mother's milk the injunction not to make oneself a nuisance when dealing with a government administration. That there is something especially strange and menacing about the castle and the Count should have become manifest to K. during his first day in the village. For instance, when he pauses at the village schoolhouse and asks the teacher whether he knows the Count, the teacher's answer takes the form of question. He says very softly, "how could I know him," and then adds in a loud voice, in French, "Keep in mind that innocent children are present." (*C*, 9) (What language do the children speak? One is reminded that the officer speaks French to the explorer in *Penal Colony*, so that the condemned man won't understand.) After that warning, K. should have recognized the need to be careful, to conform to well-worn maxims about not looking for trouble. Had he done so, perhaps he could have lived out his life in the village peacefully after all, with room and board continuing to be paid by the castle, or offered by the villagers as tribute. Instead he lurches from one misadventure to another.

Sexual desire had been gnawing at Kafka during those first months of 1922, when he was writing *The Castle.* (*D*, 412) Intense feelings of the moment often spill out onto the page as one writes. They are at work in the following scene. Olga is a village girl of whom we later learn that she offers herself to all the castle servants in her search for one particular servant whom it is crucially important for her family to propitiate. She is instinctively drawn to K.—he will be told later that she loves him—and takes him along on an errand to get beer at the Gentlemen's Inn, although its precincts are reserved to the castle gentlemen and their servants—and women who offer themselves to them. In the taproom, K. leaves her side in order to talk about Klamm to the barmaid, Frieda, "a nondescript little blonde with sad features, thin cheeks, and a surprising gaze, a gaze of exceptional superiority." (*C*, 36) She is Klamm's mistress, and she allows K. to put his eye to a secret peephole in the wall of the taproom and observe that powerful castle official. The full importance of Frieda's connection is not lost on K., though he doesn't seem to grasp the monstrousness of her indiscretion. A little later, when the landlord wants to throw out K. before closing time, which is fast approaching, he hides behind Frieda's bar, in the space where she works. Incredibly, instead of shooing him away, Frieda puts her foot on his chest and presses it as she tells the landlord that she doesn't know where K. has gone. Moments later, she is on the floor beside him:

> they embraced each other, her small body was burning in K.'s hands; they rolled a few paces in an unconscious state from which K. repeatedly but vainly tried to rescue himself, bumped dully against Klamm's door, and then lay in the small puddles of beer and of other rubbish with which the floor was covered. Hours passed there, hours breathing together with a single heartbeat, hours in which K. constantly felt that he was lost or had wandered farther into foreign lands than any human being before him....(*C*, 41)

They are still in each other's arms on the floor when Klamm is heard summoning Frieda. K. wants so badly to establish contact with Klamm that he urges her to go to him, right away, and "began to gather what was left of her blouse..." (*C*, 41) The erotic tension in this scene is matched a couple of days later in an attic room at the Bridge Inn, where Frieda and K., expelled from the Gentlemen's Inn, have found refuge:

> since the chair stood by the bed they stumbled over it and fell down. They lay there, but without abandoning themselves as fully as that time at night. She sought something and he sought something, in a fury, grimacing, they sought with their heads boring into each other's breasts; their embraces and arched bodies, far from making them forget, reminded them of their duty to keep searching, like dogs desperately pawing at the earth they pawed at each other's bodies, and then, helpless and disappointed, in an effort to catch one last bit of happiness, their tongues occasionally ran

all over each other's faces. Only weariness made them
lie still and be grateful to each other. (*C*, 45–6)

Sexual tension and barely suppressed sexual hunger are a
constant in K.'s relations with the village women, whether
Frieda, Olga, Amalia, or Peppi. Kafka may have taken note
of a similar phenomenon during the winter months he
spent with Ottla in Zürau, observing in that snowbound
and remote village peasants and their livestock huddling
in squalid promiscuity.

The intended resolution of K.'s journey, and of the
game the castle plays with him, is beyond discovery for
the simple reason that Kafka did not find it. That, rather
than physical frailty, is most likely the reason for his not
finishing his novel. At the end of the manuscript he left
in Brod's possession we find K., who has once more
been expelled from the Gentlemen's Inn, being offered
employment by Gerstäcker, a peasant who had done K. a
good turn on the first day K. spent in the village. The work
is helping with horses; Gerstäcker will provide room and
board, and also pay, if K. wants it. K. is taken aback and
says that he doesn't know anything about horses. "'That
wasn't necessary,' Gerstäcker said impatiently.'" (*C*, 316)
Now the truth dawns on K. The peasant has made the
offer because he thinks K. can help him get something
of value from one of the castle secretaries. "'Certainly,'
said Gerstäcker, 'why else would I be interested in you?'
K. laughed, took Gerstäcker's arm, and let himself be
led through the darkness." (*C*, 316) Does this signal an
epiphany? Not in the least: it is a moment of light humor,
one of many. In the next paragraph the story staggers
onward in an unknown and unpredictable direction.

Of all Kafka's works, *The Castle* is the one that least
strains the reader's credulity. It can, and in its incomplete
state probably should, be read and enjoyed as a series of

mesmerizing portraits and stories. One such story is that of Frieda and her liaison with K. She throws away everything when she gives herself to K. on the taproom floor: sex with Klamm—a pole of irresistible godlike attraction for the village women—and her unchallengeable standing as Klamm's mistress. "Klamm's proximity had made her so madly enticing." (*C*, 135) Separated from him, she withers physically. What's more, it has become apparent to her that for K. she is only a means of facilitating contacts between him and Klamm. Her judgment of K. is devastating and dismally incontrovertible:

> if Klamm wants me, you'll give me back to him, if he wants to you to stay with me, you'll stay, if he wants you to cast me out, you'll cast me out, but you're also prepared to put on a comedy, and if it's to your advantage, you'll pretend to love me, you'll try to combat his indifference by stressing your own insignificance and by shaming him with the fact that you're his successor or with tales of my confessions of love for him, which I did indeed make, and you'll ask him to take me back, but only on payment of your price; and if nothing else works, then you'll simply beg on behalf of the married couple, the K.'s. (*C*, 155–6)

What is that price? We never find out. Having gotten this far in the novel we cannot believe that it consists only of being irrefutably established in his duties of land surveyor and given a surveyor's work to do. In one of the loveliest and most wholly surprising moments in the story, Frieda says to K.: "I cannot stand this life here. If you want to hold on to me, we must leave and go somewhere else, to southern France, or to Spain." (*C*, 136) K.'s reply is equally surprising, but it doesn't explain what he is after. It is as if something invariably blocked him, or rather Kafka, when the point of revelation seems to have been reached:

> "I cannot go abroad," said K., "I came here in order to stay here," and in a contradiction he didn't bother to explain, he added as if speaking to himself: "Now what could have attracted me to this desolate land other than the desire to stay." (*C*, 136)

The incomprehension between the two is total. Frieda remembers the Bridge Inn landlady's warning her about K.: he is childishly open by nature but so different from the village people that even when he's speaking openly they can hardly bring themselves to believe him. No wonder, given K.'s sudden mood swings, self-contradictions, uncalled-for harshness and equally pointless currying of favor. His conduct is that of someone having a nervous breakdown, which was Kafka's condition when he began to write *The Castle*. This would seem to be another instance of powerful feelings experienced at the moment of composition overwhelming the text, and it is interesting to speculate about how Kafka would have reshaped K. if he had been able to finish the novel. As it is, K. engages our sympathy most fully when he is lucid, lays down his arms, and stops posing and ranting, as in his answer to Frieda, who has been taking him to task on account of his ruthless selfishness: "your entire earlier life is so submerged...that you no longer know how hard one must fight to get ahead, especially if one is coming from the depths? How one must use everything that can somehow give one hope?" (*C*, 160) Or when he tries to make Olga understand his relationship with Frieda:

> I came here voluntarily and have tied myself down here voluntarily, but everything that happened in between, and especially my future prospects—bleak

though they are, they do exist—I owe to Frieda, that simply cannot be denied. I was indeed taken on here as a surveyor, but only in appearance, they played games with me, drove me out of every house, and even today they're still playing games with me, but it's all more complicated, I have in a sense increased in girth and that already says something; trivial though this is, I do after all have a home, a position, and real work, I have a fiancée who takes over my professional work whenever I have other business to attend to, I shall marry her and join the community; I have also besides an official connection to Klamm, a personal one, of which I have admittedly not yet been able to take advantage. Now surely this is more than a little? (*C*, 198–9)

The first part of the speech is reasonable. But when K. speaks of his increased girth and plans for joining the community, he is going into a skid. As he will soon find out, Frieda is leaving him for Jeremias, one of the castle spies assigned to him as an assistant, and she will resume her duties at the Gentlemen's Inn taproom; the "home" he boasts of is a classroom in which he sleeps as the school janitor and must vacate as soon as the children arrive. As for his personal connection with Klamm—the man whose mistress Frieda had been—it is one that no decent man would claim. But a short while later, he speaks to Frieda objectively, with momentary modesty, about how he may appear to her: "I'm constantly running after things that aren't entirely comprehensible to you, that annoy you, that bring me together with people [the Barnabas family] who seem despicable to you..." (*C*, 252) K's words move her. Until, in one of the sudden reversals of which there are so many in *The Castle*, vitriol begins to flow again, she is lyrically sweet in her response:

"If only," said Frieda, slowly, calmly, almost contentedly,
as though she knew that she had merely been granted
a tiny little interlude of peace on K.'s shoulder but
intended to enjoy it to the utmost, "if only we had
gone abroad at once, that same night, we could be
somewhere else, safe, always together, your hand always
close enough for me to catch hold of; how I need your
closeness; how lost I am ever since I came to know you
without your closeness; believe me, your closeness is
the only dream that I dream, none other." (*C*, 254)

"The Cares of a Family Man," a page-and-a-half prose piece
about a curious being called Odradek, written between 1914
and 1917, and included in the collection *A Country Doctor*,
contains a useful warning. The narrator, a "paterfamilias" (a
better translation in this instance of *Hausvater* than "family
man" used in the Schocken Books edition), is speaking
about Odradek:

Some say that the word Odradek is of Slavonic origin,
and try to account for it on that basis. Others again
believe it to be of Germanic origin, only influenced
by Slavonic. The uncertainty of both interpretations allows one to assume with justice that neither
is accurate, especially as neither of them provides an
intelligent meaning of the word. (*CS*, 427–8)

The obvious preliminary question should be: why does
the origin of that word Odradek matter?[1] Kafka's exegetes do

---

1   In fact, the origin is clearly Slavonic. *Odradek* is a word that doesn't
exist in the Czech language. However, its cognate "*odradit*" is a
Czech verb that among other things means "to discourage." The
broad hint has not discouraged Kafkologists. The search continues.
(cf. Bi, 342)

not pause to ask it. Instead, they have debated the derivation of the name, subjecting Kafka's little text to the same heavy artillery used to storm the meaning of *The Trial*. Clues have been sought in Kafka's biography (he wrote "Cares of a Family Man" in the little house in Alchimistengasse, the first house he had ever had to himself), and through the application of a Lacanian cocktail of psychoanalysis, structuralism, and linguistics. (*Bi*, 342–3) Brod himself has suggested that, since he has no "fixed abode," Odradek may symbolize the Wandering Jew. (*B*, 135)

The paterfamilias has this to say about Odradek's nature:

> At first glance...[Odradek] looks like a star-shaped spool for thread....But it is not only a spool, for a wooden crossbar sticks out of the middle of the star, and another small rod is joined to that at a right angle. By means of this latter rod on one side and one of the points of the star on the other, the whole thing can stand upright as if on two legs....the whole thing looks senseless enough, but in its own way perfectly finished....closer scrutiny is impossible, since Odradek is extraordinarily nimble and can never be laid hold of. (*CS*, 428)

We learn that Odradek does get around. You find him in the garret, in the stairway, in lobbies. When he isn't seen, presumably the reason is that he has been visiting other houses, but he always returns to "our" house again. Because he is so diminutive you can't help treating him "rather like a child." You don't put difficult questions to him, but you can ask his name—he answers Odradek—and you can ask him where he lives. The reply to that is, "No fixed abode." There are unasked questions that trouble the paterfamilias: Can Odradek possibly die? "Anything that dies," he speculates, "has had some aim in life, some kind of activity, which has worn out; but that does not apply to Odradek." (*CS*, 429)

Is the paterfamilias then to suppose that Odradek will not die, will still be rolling down the stairs under the feet of his children, and his children's children? Odradek does not seem to harm anyone, "but the idea that he is likely to survive me I find almost painful." (*CS*, 428)

It is small wonder that exegesis does not seem to have yielded an intelligent meaning. Vladimir Nabokov held that the only real readers are those who reread—a dictum that has never been truer than when applied to Kafka's works. The significance of Kafka's little prose piece is in the pleasure that a real reader experiences by surrendering to Kafka's words; a pleasure not dissimilar from that found in mouthing certain lines of poetry, for instance, "Charm'd magic casements, opening on the foam / Of perilous seas, in faery lands forlorn." It is a pleasure that brings with it the sense of being in the presence of a mystery. "Odradek," Benjamin wrote in an essay commemorating the tenth anniversary of Kafka's death, "is the form which things assume in oblivion." (*Ill*, 133) We know immediately that he was right, although we would be hard put to explain why or to interpret what he said. Some things cannot be explained.

If there is an "intelligent meaning" to be found in "The Judgment," *In the Penal Colony*, *The Metamorphosis*, *Amerika*, *The Trial*, or *The Castle*, it is the response that these works evoke in the reader. When the window looking out on the execution scene is flung open in *The Trial*, K. sees in it a "human figure, faint and insubstantial at that distance and at that height." That vision and the butcher's knife are all that is left to him. He has not penetrated to the judge who condemned him or to the high court, he has not been able to present the arguments that might prove

that, although even if "[l]ogic is doubtless unshakable...
it cannot withstand a man who wants to go on living."
(*T*, 228) The obverse of the universal yearning for human
solidarity is an equally universal truth, one that the Narrator
in Proust's great novel, *In Search of Lost Time*, discovers
when a celebrated doctor gives short shrift to the Narrator's
grandmother, who has just suffered a stroke. The doctor
is in a hurry. He doesn't want to be late for an official
reception. The Narrator concludes: *chaque personne est bien
seule*, each person is completely alone. It may be that Joseph
K. discovers that truth in his last moment of consciousness,
and that so do the other great victims in Kafka's fiction:
Georg, at the moment he cries out "Dear parents, I have
loved you all the same," and Gregor, when "his head sank
to the floor of its own accord and from his nostrils came
the last faint flicker of breath." It may be the secret behind
the explorer's anomie.

Battered and bruised, Karl Rossmann and K. also suffer
from loneliness and nostalgia, inevitable afflictions of
protagonists of road novels and knights and heroes who
set out on a quest. Both Karl and K. are enigmas, Kafka
having arrested their development by abandoning them
prematurely. But road novels do not end neatly, unless
the author arranges for the protagonist to die, or to
have him reach his Ithaca or Colchis. In the latter case,
a new adventure will surely beckon, but that can be left
for another day. The author can also, if he dares, declare
victory. That is what Witold Gombrowicz did with his
Ferdydurke. Unable to find an ending that satisfied him for
that story, he consulted a young chambermaid. She told
him to put a piece of doggerel after the last sentence of the
novel and call it quits, that being the way that Polish fairy
tales sometimes end. Gombrowicz did just that, drawing
on a Polish nobleman's inexhaustible reserve of arrogance
and sangfroid. The doggerel is almost untranslatable, but

a reasonable English approximation runs as follows: "Basta and pop! Whoever has read this is a sop."[2]

Kafka brought *Amerika* and *The Castle* as far as he could and accepted defeat.

---

2 In Polish: **Koniec i bomba/ A kto czytał, ten trąba!**

Key to References

A   Kafka, Franz, *Amerika*, trans. Willa and Edwin Muir (New
        York: Schocken Books, 1974).

B   Brod, Max, *Franz Kafka—A Biography*, trans. G.
        Humphreys Roberts and Richard Winston (New York:
        Da Capo, 1995).

Bi   Binder, Hartmut (ed.), *Kafka-Handbuch*, vol. II (Stuttgart:
        Alfred Kröner Verlag, 1979).

C   Kafka, Franz, *The Castle*, trans. Mark Harman (New York:
        Schocken Books, 1996).

CS   Kafka, Franz, *The Complete Stories*, ed. Nahum Glatzer
        (New York: Schocken Books, 1971).

D   Kafka, Franz, *Diaries 1910–1923*, ed. Max Brod, trans.
        Joseph Kresh and Martin Greenberg (New York: Schocken
        Books, 1975).

Ill   Benjamin, Walter, *Illuminations: Essays and Reflections*, ed.
        Hannah Arendt, trans. Harry Zohn (New York: Schocken
        Books, 1969).

J   Janouch, Gustav, *Conversations with Kafka*, trans.
        Goronway Ress (New York: New Directions, 1971).

L   Kafka, Franz, *Letters to Friends, Family, and Editors,* ed. Max Brod, trans. Richard and Clara Winston (New York: Schocken Books, 1977).

LF   Kafka, Franz, *Letters to Felice*, ed. Erich Heller and Jürgen Born, trans. James Stern and Elisabeth Duckworth (New York: Schocken Books, 1973).

LM   Kafka, Franz, *Letters to Milena*, trans. Philip Boehm (New York: Schocken Books, 1990).

LO   Kafka, Franz, *Letters to Ottla and the Family*, ed. N. N. Glatzer, trans. Richard and Clara Winston (New York: Schocken Books, 1982).

RK   Anderson, Mark (ed.), *Reading Kafka: Prague, Politics and the Fin de Siècle* (New York: Schocken Books, 1989).

S   Kafka, Franz, *Letter to His Father*, trans. Ernst Kaiser and Eithne Wilkens, rev. Arthur S. Wensinger, in Kafka, Franz, *The Sons* (New York: Schocken Books, 1989).

T   Kafka, Franz, *The Trial*, trans. Willa and Edwin Muir, rev. E. M. Butler (New York: Schocken Books, 1974)

The quotations in my text are taken from the editions listed above, but I have silently emended them when it seemed appropriate to achieve greater clarity or accuracy.

Selected Bibliography

The German edition of Kafka's works I have most often consulted is *Gesammelte Werke*, ed. Max Brod (Frankfurt: Fischer Taschenbuch Verlag, 1996), which includes Kafka's diaries and letters to addressees other than Felice and Milena. I have also consulted *Franz Kafka: Briefe an Felice und andere Korrespondenz aus dar Verlobungszeit*, ed. Erich Heller and Jürgen Born (Frankfurt: Fischer Taschenbuch Verlag, 2003), and *Franz Kafka: Briefe an Milena*, ed. Jürgen Born and Michael Müller (Frankfurt: Fischer Taschenbuch Verlag, 1986).

Literature about Kafka and his life is a dense forest. In addition to works referred to above, I have found most valuable the following:

Boa, Elizabeth *Kafka: Gender, Class and Race in the Letters and Fictions*. Oxford, 1966. As the title makes clear, a specialized study, but lively and informative.

Born, Jürgen, ed. *Kafkas Bibliothek—Ein beschreibendes Verzeichnis mit einem Index aller in Kafka's Schriften erwähnten Bücher, Zeitschriften and Zeitschriftenbeitrage; zusammengestellt unter Mitarbeit von Michael Antreter und Jon Shepherd* (Frankfurt: S. Fischer Verlag, 1990). This is a fascinating descriptive catalog of books in Kafka's library.

Calasso, Roberto, *K.*, trans. Geoffrey Brock (New York: Alfred A. Knopf, 2005). An imaginative and eloquent reading of *The Trial* and *The Castle*.

Canetti, Elias, *Kafka's Other Trial: The Letters to Felice*, trans. Christopher Middleton (New York: Schocken Books, 1974). A sensitive and astute study of the letters by the Nobel Prize–winning novelist, in whose opinion the "trial" at the Askanische Hof was retried in *The Trial*.

Citati, Pietro, *Kafka*, London, trans. Raymond Rosenthal (London: Secker & Warburg, 1990). An elegant and sensitive biography.

Gilman, Sander L. *Franz Kafka: The Jewish Patient* (New York: Routledge, 1995). A brilliant and erudite survey of European anti-Semitism and anti-Semitic stereotypes, and the way in which they affected Kafka's life and works.

Northey, Anthony. *Kafka's Relatives: Their Lives and His Writing* (New Haven: Yale University Press, 1991). Traces the migrations and adventures of the members of Kafka and Löwy families, and the use Kafka may have made of them.

Pawel, Ernst, *The Nightmare of Reason: A Life of Franz Kafka* (New York: Noonday Press, Farrar Straus Giroux, 1984). Still the best general biography of Kafka.

Stölzl, Christoph. *Kafka's böses Böhmen: Zur Socialgeschichte eines Prager Juden* (Munich: edition text + kritik, 1975). Unavailable in English but indispensable as an introduction to the social context in which Kafka grew up and worked.

Unseld, Joachim, *Franz Kafka: A Writer's Life*, trans. Paul F. Dworak (Riverside: Ariadne, 1994). Traces the complex history of the publication of Kafka's works.

Wagenbach, Klaus, *Kafka*, trans. Ewald Osers (London: Haus Publishing, 2003). Originally published in 1964, it has withstood the test of time and is still among the best short biographies of the author.

Use of German place-names

Kafka used German place-names and street names in his diaries and correspondence. I have followed his usage. The current Czech equivalents are set forth below:

Alchimistengasse	Zlatá ulička
Altstädter Ring	Staroměstské náměstí
Bilekgasse	Ulička Bilkova
Ferdinand-Karls-Universität	Univerzita Karlova v Praze (Charles University in Prague)
Friedland	Frýdlant
Graben	Na Příkopě
Karlsbrücke	Karluv Most
Lange Gasse	Dlouhá
Heinrichgasse	Jindřisšká
Kleinseite	Malá Strana

Marienbad	Mariánske Lázne
Moldau	Vltava
Niklasstrasse	Parízská
Podiebrad	Poděbrady
Rathausgasse	Ulička Radnice
Reichenberg	Liberic
Schelesen	Želízy
Spindelmühle	Špindlerův Mlýn
Triesch	Třešt
Woßek	Osek
Zuckmantel	Slaté hory
Zürau	Siřem
Woßek	Osek
Zeltnergasse	Celetná

Important Dates in Franz Kafka's Life

1883   July 3: FK born in Prague, son of Herman Kafka and Julie, née Löwy.

1889–93   Attends elementary school.

1889   October 29: birth of his favorite sister Ottla, youngest daughter of Herman and Julie.

1893–1901 Attends secondary school.

1897   Anti-Semitic riots in Prague.

1901   Enters university and settles on the study of law.

1902   Summer vacation with Dr. Siegfried Löwy (the "country doctor") in Triesch. October: first meeting with Max Brod.

1904   Begins writing "Description of a Struggle," earliest surviving work.

1905   Vacation in Zuckmantel, Silesia. First love affair, with the "mature woman."

1906   June 18: Doctor of Law degree. October: begins one-year training period first at the civil high court and then at the criminal court.

1907–8	Work at the Prague branch of Assicurazioni Generali.
1908	March: publishes eight prose pieces in the review *Hyperion*. Enters the partially government-owned Workers' Accident Insurance Institute.
1909	Begins keeping diaries.
1910	Promoted to the position of *Konzipist* (Chief Clerk) at the Insurance Institute.
1911	Investment in the asbestos factory owned by his brother-in-law. Friendship with the Yiddish actor Yitzhak Löwy. Growing interest in Yiddish theater and Judaism.
1912	February 18: introduces a reading by Yitzhak Löwy of Yiddish poetry delivering his address on Yiddish language. August: prepares for publication his first book, a collection of short prose pieces, *Meditation* (*Betrachtung*); meets Felice Bauer. Beginning in September: begins correspondence with Felice Bauer, writes "The Judgment," *The Metamorphosis*, and begins *Amerika*.
1913	January: interrupts writing of *Amerika*. Extensive correspondence with Felice; sees her in Berlin three times; beginning of acquaintance with Grete Bloch. Travels via Trieste, Venice, and Verona to Riva. Liaison with "Swiss girl." Promoted to position of vice-secretary at the Institute.
1914	June: official engagement to Felice. July: confrontation at the Askanischer Hof;

engagement is broken; travels with Ernst
Weiss and Weiss's mistress to Travemünde and
Marielyst.
August 2: Germany enters the war.
Later in August begins work on *The Trial*.
October and through the end of the year:
works on *Trial*, writes *In the Penal Colony* and
a chapter of *Amerika*.

1915   January: stops work on *The Trial*. First
        meeting with Felice Bauer since the break in
        July 1914; two more meetings follow, in May
        (Grete also present), and June.
        November: book publication of *The
        Metamorphosis*.

1916   July through November: meetings with
        Felice; in July in Marienbad.
        October: "The Judgment" published in book
        form.
        November: begins to use the little house in
        Alchimistengasse that Ottla has rented. The
        stories written there and in 1917 will be
        published in 1920 as *A Country Doctor*.

1917   July: second engagement to Felice; Felice and
        FK make courtesy visits to family and friends
        in Prague.
        August: first major hemorrhage.
        September: diagnosis of tuberculosis. Goes
        to stay with Ottla in Zürau, where he will
        remain until April 1918.
        December: second engagement to Felice is
        broken.

1918   May: FK resumes work at the Institute.
        October: sick with Spanish influenza and
        double pneumonia.

November: resumes work at the Institute, but falls sick again; at the end of November, his mother takes him to Schelesen, where he stays at Pension Stüdl; will remain there until March 1919. Meets Julie Wohryzek

1919   Spring and summer: sees Julie Wohryzek in Prague and becomes engaged to her. November: wedding to Julie is postponed. In Schelesen, with Max Brod. Writes *Letter to His Father*. *In the Penal Colony* is published in book form.

1920   January 1: FK becomes secretary of the Institute.
April: on medical leave in Merano. Writes first letter to Milena Jesenská.
May: publication of *A Country Doctor*.
June 29–July 4: visits Milena in Vienna. July: breaks engagement to Julie.
August 14–5: meets Milena in Gmünd.
November: violent anti-Semitic riots in Prague.
Winter: break with Milena; FK goes on medical leave to Matliary.

1921   August: returns from Matliary.
October: gives all his diaries to Milena, and resumes keeping a diary.
November until the end of the year: gravely ill and mostly bedridden, receives medical treatment at parents' apartment. Visited there several times by Milena.

1922   Mid-January: nervous breakdown. January 27, goes to Spindlermühle for about three weeks, and begins to write *The Castle*. February– July: writes "A Hunger Artist," and "The Investigations of a Dog." End of June: goes to

stay with Ottla in Planá, where he will remain
until September.
July: retires from the Institute.
End of August: nervous breakdown.
October: "The Hunger Artist" published in a
review.
November: abandons work on *The Castle*.

1923   Winter and spring: mostly bedridden; resumes
studies of Hebrew.
July: on vacation in Müritz on the Baltic sea
with his sister Elli, meets Dora Diamant.
September: moves with Dora to Berlin.
October–December: writes "The Burrow."

1924   Health deteriorates rapidly.
March 17: Returns with Brod to Prague.
Staying at parents' apartment, writes
"Josephine the Singer, or the Mouse Folk."
End of March: accompanied by Dora, enters
Sanatorium Wiener Wald in lower Austria;
diagnosis of tuberculosis of the larynx.
April 19: accompanied by Dora, enters
sanatorium in Kierling, near Vienna. Corrects
galleys for the collection of stories *A Hunger
Artist*.
June 3: FK dies at age of forty.
June 11: burial in the Strasnice Jewish
Cemetary.

Acknowledgments

I wish to express my profound gratitude to the following:

My dear friends Joel Conarroe and Donald Hall, for reading an early version of this book and offering invaluable suggestions and encouragement.

My publisher, James Atlas, for inspiring me to write this book, and my editor, John Oakes, for his patient care for my text.

My dear friend, Jeffrey P. Cunard, for leading me through the thicket of intellectual property law.

My dear friend Deborah M. Lizasoain, whose eagle eye caught more mistakes in the successive versions of my text than I have had the courage to count.

Credits